Life with My Mary

JOSEPH A. BREIG

THE BRUCE PUBLISHING COMPANY
MILWAUKEE

Dedication

I HAVE NOT DONE JUSTICE to my wife in this book. The reason is simple: it is impossible. I cannot express what she has been to me in our twenty-five years of togetherness in sacramental marriage. This story, however, perhaps will give the reader some faint notion of what is in my heart as I dedicate this volume to all good wives, and very specially to:

MARY MY WIFE

LIFE WITH MY MARY

ON A GOLDEN AUTUMN EVENING in my twentieth year, I was sauntering, with a sophomore's air, across the campus of the University of Notre Dame. To a classmate who accompanied me, I was expounding some thought which I imagined to be profound.

So absorbed was I that I hardly noticed the hundreds of other students who were also crossing the campus, not strolling as I was, but walking purposefully. Nor was I aware of the fact that when we came to a fork in the path, my companion put a hand on my arm and guided me to the right.

Suddenly, though, my flow of words halted in midsentence. I had become conscious that my friend had said something. What he had said was, "Let's go to the novena."

I looked at him sharply. "Did you say novena?"

"Yes."

"What novena?"

"The novena for a happy marriage."

I chuckled, and resumed my stroll. "Don't you know I don't go with girls? Why should I pray for a happy marriage?"

His grip tightened on my arm. "What of it? Pray for something else."

Now I told the whole truth. "I don't want to go to a novena. I don't mind once — but that nine-day business is too long for me."

"Look," he said. "It's only half an hour every evening. What's half an hour?"

"I just don't feel like going," I told him.

"The novena's in honor of your patron," he argued quietly. "St. Joseph. You ought to go."

Now I hesitated. I did not want to seem rude to my patron saint.

My friend drove in the clincher. "Come along this once," he said. "You don't have to finish the novena if you don't want to."

"Oh, all right," I consented. "Let's go."

We quickened our pace and went toward Sacred Heart Church, on the quadrangle hard by the Administration Building with its famous golden statue of our Lady, atop the Golden Dome.

The Church of the Sacred Heart is a soaring French Gothic structure, erected, with magnificent courage, at a time when the Holy Cross Fathers, who founded Notre Dame, were nearly penniless.

Ordinarily, the church is hushed, almost sleepy under the benign gaze of a statue of the Virgin which stands bathed in blue light in a niche high above the sanctuary.

Tonight, the nave was filled with young men whose deep voices, singing a hymn, reverberated through the arches.

I had no intention of returning for the devotions after that first night. But I did. I came back every evening until the novena was finished. I don't know why.

A couple of months later, I went home for Christmas vacation and saw, in my father's store, the girl who was to be my wife.

I supposed at first that she was a customer. I was obscurely happy to learn that she was a clerk, and could be seen there every day.

I nearly haunted the store after that. I struck up an acquaintance. I protested when I saw her carrying slightly heavy things. I took such loads from her hands and placed them where she wanted them.

I was pleased to learn that her name was Mary.

I disapproved when I discovered that she walked home alone after sunset. This wouldn't do, I told her. I insisted upon seeing her home through the early dusk.

Each evening, she parted from me at her front door, went swiftly up the steps, and went in, while I turned away.

But she began putting her arm in mine occasionally as we walked along.

I did not really realize that Mary was only seventeen and that to her I seemed a strange being from another world — a college boy home on vacation, the son of her employer.

Nevertheless, one evening she consented to eat a sundae with me in the Sugar Bowl. And at last she agreed to ask her mother whether she might go to a movie with me.

Her mother said yes, and on the appointed evening I appeared at the Hoffman home, slicked and shined and pressed and brushed.

Mary's mother had a genius for putting people at ease. I discovered in five minutes that my future mother-in-law — of whom I did not then think in that way — was a remarkable woman.

She opened the door for me and chatted just long enough.

Then she called upstairs to Mary to hurry, and Mary came down the steps. She was a vision to me.

We went to another movie the night before I was returning to Notre Dame. I told Mary haltingly that I hated to leave. She pressed my arm with her hand.

At her home after the movie, she stood on the porch steps while I made conversation, trying to delay the moment of parting. I stood below her on the sidewalk.

Presently I fell silent and stood looking up at her dumbly. She hesitated. She glanced quickly to right and left.

She leaned down swiftly, kissed me, turned, and fled into the house.

A day later, I was strolling again on the campus of Notre Dame, stopping all my friends and saying proudly, "Shake hands with a man in love."

Then I regaled them with descriptions of Mary.

They listened sympathetically, shook their heads, and said to one another, "Imagine. Breig. The guy who never went out with girls. The guy we couldn't drag within a mile of any of the receptions at St. Mary's. The guy we *did* drag to the dance downtown that time."

They had indeed once dragged me to a dance.

They had pounced upon me, half a dozen of them, and put me into a tuxedo several sizes too small, and into dress shoes several sizes too large. And they had taken me to the dance by main force.

In the ballroom, they had made it their fiendish business to bring the prettiest girls to the corner where I cowered, to introduce them to me, and to suggest that they wanted to dance with me.

All that I could do was to blush, bow awkwardly, take each

girl's hand while the right sleeve of my jacket rose almost to my elbow, and point dumbly to my oversized shoes, stuffed with paper to hold them on my feet.

"How can I dance in these?" I mumbled, and thus escaped the dreadful prospect of venturing on the dance floor with an utterly strange girl in my arms.

Now these same young men stared at me, flabbergasted, as I stopped them on the campus or in the residence halls with my strange announcement: "Shake hands with a man in love!"

Mary and I exchanged a few strained, almost formal letters — but letters with a youthful touch of embarrassed warmth in them — during the next semester.

Then I came home for the too-brief Easter vacation. We saw each other a few times, and I went back to Notre Dame.

At last I was home for the long summer vacation.

Now my courtship — although I did not think of it as that — started in earnest.

Mary had left my father's employment. She had become a shoe clerk.

So I became interested in shoes. I became a connoisseur of shoes. And I became a connoisseur of the habits of the owner of this particular shoe store.

I knew almost to the minute when he would go out for lunch, and when return.

I knew also — or I soon discovered — that he was a sympathetic chap who, when there were few customers, would tell Mary to leave fifteen minutes early in the evening if I put in my appearance at that time.

Thus did the courtship proceed.

I began to become a tolerated nuisance around Mary's home. I invented reasons, too, for inviting her often to my home for dinner.

One evening an incident cemented me solidly in the amused affections of Mary's father and mother.

I had read somewhere that the shell of an egg is so strong, end for end, that it can be squeezed with all one's strength in the hand, and not break, so long as the pressure is not exerted on the sides.

I mentioned this one evening to Mary's parents. Her father snorted. Her mother said it seemed very odd to her. I turned to Mary. "If you'll lend me an egg, I'll show you."

She told me not to be silly. I insisted. At last her mother, with a laugh, said, "Give him an egg."

I stood in their living room squeezing the egg in my right hand until the knuckles were white.

Nothing happened.

Mary's father gave a little cluck of astonishment. Her mother watched me apprehensively.

Emboldened by success, I took the egg in both hands and brought pressure to bear.

Still nothing happened.

"Watch," I told them. "You wouldn't believe how strong an egg is."

I sat down and put my hands, holding the egg, between my knees.

Mary said protestingly, "Joe — don't!"

"It won't break," I assured her.

I applied pressure with my knees and hands — more and more pressure.

The eggshell collapsed, and its contents flew about the room. Some struck the walls, some the ceiling. Some lodged in Mary's mother's hair.

I sat there speechless.

I stared dumbly at Mary's father, and at her mother.

Her mother collapsed in helpless laughter. Her father started to give forth short, tentative chuckles.

In a moment, we were all laughing, and I think that from that moment, I began to be a member of the family.

The summer vacation passed swiftly, in a kind of golden glow.

Often I borrowed my father's battered old car so that Mary and I could ride through the Pennsylvania hills, laughing like children.

Once we coasted down a long winding hill, crying out with joy as we swung around curves and roller-coasted over humps in the road.

Suddenly Mary shut her mouth and put her hand to it. Her face was so alarmed that I braked the car to a stop.

She opened her mouth, closed it, opened it again, and at last spoke.

"I swallowed a bug," she said.

She looked reproachfully at me when I laughed.

Another time, as I returned Mary to her home, I got out of the car gallantly and walked around to open the door on her side for her.

I glanced into the back seat. We had been accompanied all afternoon by a box of dynamite sticks.

I protested vigorously to my father about that. He pooh-poohed me. "Dynamite can't explode without a percussion cap," he informed me.

I was not mollified.

What he was doing with dynamite, I do not know. But he was a man who could and would turn his hand to any task. He was carpenter, plumber, electrician, salesman, merchant, almost anything.

Suddenly, much too soon, the summer vacation was over, and again I was walking the campus of Notre Dame.

The first faint signs of the approaching Great Depression were beginning to appear. My mother's letters told me that my father's business was declining alarmingly.

I had had enough of college anyhow. I had decided after graduating from high school that I wanted to be a newspaperman, and I had no particular need of a degree. In fact, I had signed as a special student at Notre Dame so that I could take whatever courses I wished — whatever I thought would be useful to me in journalism.

Now I decided to let my junior year be my last, and to go home and go to work. I did so.

I resumed my courtship of Mary at once.

The police department acquired a proprietary interest in our romance. One morning Officer Tackle McIntyre, so known from his football days, telephoned me at the office of the home-town newspaper, where I had got a job.

"You there?" asked Tackle.

"I'm answering the phone," I told him tartly.

"Just wondered," he said, with a chuckle. "Thought maybe something happened to you. How come your Dad's car's still parked in front of your girl's house?"

I had said good night to Mary, walked past the car, and trudged home afoot.

This began to happen so often that Tackle McIntyre's voice

turned weary when he telephoned. "Look, Joe — will you *please* take that car home with you in the evenings? We're getting tired watching it for you."

I felt that this was an exaggeration. The auto was too ancient to tempt thieves.

Now I was beginning to find even brief separations from Mary almost unbearable.

Once, I recall, she went to a town some miles distant to visit her grandmother. I fretted it out for a day. Then I asked Dad whether he needed his car. He did.

Our newspaper owned a dilapidated sedan, minus the door on the driver's side. It was used for delivering papers.

I asked the newspaper owner, then Robert Slough, whether he would lend me the old thing to visit my girl. "Sure," he said heartily. "Take it."

I got caught in a blizzard coming home, and nearly found myself marooned on snow-buried country roads. But my visit with Mary had been worth it a hundred times over.

2

NEITHER MARY nor I can remember when I gave her the engagement ring. Why we have forgotten the details of that moment, we cannot imagine. But we have.

It was an inexpensive ring, not in the least impressive. My salary was small, and my father's business was still falling off. It was necessary to be economical.

More than once in the years since, I have asked Mary to let me replace the ring with something much better. She always looks at me as if I have taken leave of my senses, and says gently, "This is my engagement ring. I don't want another one; I want this one."

As I remember, the engagement ring and the wedding ring were bought together from a wholesale firm with which my father did business.

Mary and I had never had expensive tastes. We had been reared simply. We grew up, so to speak, in both the past and the future — in agricultural America and in industrial America.

Our town was a blending of the two. It is called Vandergrift, after its founder, a former river-boat captain who became wealthy in steel production.

Vandergrift for years was famed as Pennsylvania's first

"model town." It was created by the steel firm that Captain Vandergrift headed, but it owed its conception to Vandergrift's general manager, George G. McMurtry, who had seen model industrial communities in Germany.

Before any house was built, Vandergrift was designed by Frederick Law Olmstead, architect of the Chicago World's Fair of 1893. All the streets curved according to the contour of the land, which was a kind of hilly peninsula made by a broad bend in the Kiskiminetas River.

In my childhood in Vandergrift, virtually everybody was a newcomer. The community consisted mainly of young married couples who had come in from the farms roundabout, attracted by the good wages in the steel plant. The population then was two thousand, if you were a Vandergrift patriot; rather less, if you were a statistical realist.

Both Mary and I were born in little rented houses, she on Custer Avenue, I on Farragut. The world into which we came was a world of horses and wagons, buggies and surreys; of a town baseball team, a fair ground, and harness racing.

Perhaps the town's proudest boast was its volunteer fire department, of which, if I may say so with pardonable pride, my father was the first chief.

Every fire was a town event, dutifully attended by everybody. The fire engines were drawn to the scene by galloping horses, which then were unhitched and returned to their stables. After the fire was extinguished, dozens of willing hands laid hold of immense loops of rope and pulled the fire equipment back to the firehouse by sheer man power.

It was a world of church-lawn fetes, of hell-and-damnation preaching, of bustles on the women and ferocious mustaches on the men; of derbies and plumed hats and peg-top trousers;

of runaway horses, blacksmith shops, and the settlement of arguments by fisticuffs.

And yet it was a world economically dominated by the big steel plant which roared and crashed and groaned, day and night, within sight and easy sound of the streets where Mary and I played.

Almost everybody worked in the steel plant, and from its siren came the demoniac howling which woke everybody every time there was a fire, followed by the mournful short and long blasts which told everybody where the fire was.

I like to indulge in the fancy of wondering whether I ever saw Mary in my boyhood. Probably not; our streets were several blocks apart, and in those days it was wise for a boy not to venture far from his own neighborhood. Each street had its gang which jealously guarded its own preserves.

Vandergrift was an intensely Protestant community in those days. Protestant churches were everywhere. There was only one Catholic church, a poor little wooden building where Mary and I were baptized, where we were taken for Mass on Sundays, and where we went to Sunday School to learn by rote the gigantic central truths of our Faith.

"Who made you?" "God made me."

"Why did God make you?" "God made me to know Him, to love Him, to serve Him, and to be happy forever with Him in heaven."

"Is there but one God?" "Yes, there *is* but one God."

And so on.

Not until many years later did the enormous significance of those parroted lessons begin to penetrate into our consciousness, to be profoundly realized.

Ours was a simple world. I recall that our family extracted

reiterated pleasure for years out of an answer given by my younger brother Robert when he was asked in Sunday School to repeat the Fourth Commandment. He said, "The Fourth Commandment means that parents must obey their children."

Mary, I am sure, had no trouble with her non-Catholic classmates in the public grade schools, where I must have been in the fourth or fifth grade when she was in the first.

Mary is a quiet person. I was not, and am not.

Even in those early years, I rose in class and corrected the teacher on the rare occasions when she made some misstatement about what Catholics believed. I earned the cordial dislike of my muscularly Protestant fellow pupils, and on occasion, had to outrun posses of Protestant boys.

I could run as fast as they, and I could run longer. I can still remember the strange terror of hearing behind me the shouts of a dozen or more boys, "Get that mick!"

I do not mean to suggest that there was no fault on my side. I may have seemed fairly insufferable, although I was merely trying to defend my convictions from gross misrepresentations. But I will not deny that I may have defended them with more vigor than understanding of the other fellow.

My closest friend for a while at that time was a Jewish lad named Robert Einstein. We shared a common misery; both of us were ostracized and isolated from the group. I felt a special sympathy for Robert, because whereas I was fairly sturdy, he was frail.

I do not think that either of us was conscious of what it was that drew, or rather drove, us together; but subconsciously we knew. We were companions in a kind of unspoken and only half-realized sorrow. Each of us carried the cross of being different; and in childhood, that is a heavy cross.

I must note here, however, that not long afterward I formed a fast friendship with a Protestant boy, whose name, I believe, was Robert Allen. His father, it seems to me, was superintendent of schools, although for all that mattered to me, he might have been President of Saskatchewan, if there is any such thing. Robert and I spent endless hours watching a war between a colony of black ants and a colony of red ants, both of which had their underground cities in his lawn.

I mention these matters only to illustrate the atmosphere in which Mary and I, Catholics in an overwhelmingly and belligerently Protestant town, grew up.

Let it not be supposed that I bear the slightest resentment. I endured some childish cruelties, yes, and occasionally an adult uncharity; but I could fill a volume with the kindnesses that were shown to me, and I am sure that Mary could do likewise.

One shining example was Mr. Whitworth. We called him, we children, Old Man Whitworth, in capital letters; not irreverently, but reverently. He was president of the town's bank; he was then, I suppose, in his sixties; he took a long walk every day, swinging his cane, but he never failed to stop and talk with the children he met.

I shall forever be grateful to him because he discovered that I loved to read, and promptly commanded me to come to his big house, where he piled my arms with books about Tom Swift and the Rover Boys and the like. His stock of such volumes seemed inexhaustible, and for years I borrowed from his library.

Our town at that time was a town of horses. They pulled

the delivery wagons on weekdays and on Sundays the surreys.

I recall the strange feeling of wonder with which I once beheld Mr. McGeary, whom I knew as a real estate man, competing in a harness race at a Kiskiminetas Valley Fair. I think too of Mr. Wagner, the iceman, swaying on his high wagon seat, and distributing olives to children who clustered about.

I thought he was handing out candy, and I shall never forget my incredulity and shock at my first taste of an olive. I slunk away and spat it out; I could not let Mr. Wagner think that his gift was unappreciated.

I remember another kind of shock, too. Once I was trapped in an alley in front of a team of runaway horses. Fleeing with all the strength of my short legs, I reached the intersection and flung myself out of danger an instant before the great hooves thundered past me.

Often I stood watching the blacksmith, whose name, appropriately, was Smith. I paid little attention to the lurid oaths he uttered while shoeing horses; I was entirely fascinated by the flaming forge, the smoke, and the red-hot steel which Mr. Smith shaped so expertly under his hammer. Yet his profanity found its way into my subconscious, because when I was coming out of ether after an operation for removal of my tonsils, I seemed to hear myself cursing the surgeon like a trooper.

To this day, I do not know whether the fearful words really were uttered, or whether I merely half-dreamed that I was shouting them. Neither the surgeon nor my mother — who was at my bedside — ever mentioned the matter, and I was far too embarrassed to ask whether they had heard the oaths that had swirled in my mind.

Our little world of Vandergrift changed with astounding rapidity. Automobiles, at first called horseless carriages, began to appear on the dusty streets, their exhausts clattering and emitting fumes. The Industrial Revolution was beginning to be felt in our home town.

In a way, it was a pity. The children of the future were not to know the heart-stirring thrill of waking before dawn to hear the rumbling of circus wagons being unloaded from freight cars at the railroad depot. They were not to stand almost within arm's length as elephants shuffled past in parade, trunk-to-tail. The arrival of machinery meant the departure of much romance.

My father bought a secondhand Cadillac. It had a one-cylinder engine, with an enormous flywheel under the front seat. He paid fifty dollars for it. Because there was no fuel pump, the Cadillac would not go up hills frontward; my father had to turn it and back up.

I remember how angry I was because larger boys would jump on when we started, ride until we came to a hill, jump off, run ahead of us to the top, and stand jeering, waiting for us. I was angry because I thought they were jeering my father. He explained, smiling, that they were jeering the car.

Every Sunday, everybody who had some kind of automobile dressed up in dusters and went for a ride. The ride was four miles long round trip — to the end of what was called the Brick Road, and return.

Once, riding along, we missed my brother. My father turned the Cadillac and retraced his course. Half a mile back, we found the missing lad, serenely trudging along with his hand in the hand of a man who had found him unhurt beside the road where he had fallen out.

Such was Vandergrift in those days. But down beside the Kiskiminetas River, the steel works clanked and banged and roared, producing the kind of material that was to change our world and all the rest of the world.

We did not begin to realize how wide and deep that transformation was until America entered World War I, and steel was hurled in countless tons along the Western Front.

The young men of Vandergrift went away to war, simple and unspoiled. They came back, and they were not the same, many of them.

Prohibition contributed the final touch. The young men and young women began to carry flasks, and to paw one another, and to dance immodestly, and all that. Our town had a transition to go through, and the transition period left a lot of casualties in its wake.

Mary's father worked sometimes in Vandergrift, and sometimes in Canton, Ohio; and Mary as a child gravitated between public schools in Vandergrift and a parish school in Canton.

I attended the public schools until the seventh grade. For two years thereafter I was at St. Vincent's Prep School in Latrobe, Pennsylvania. I can never be sufficiently eloquent about the profound influence for good which the Benedictine monks exercised upon me during those two years.

I returned then to Vandergrift Public High School, from where I went to the University of Notre Dame and to the novena for a happy marriage in which I unwillingly participated.

And so we come back to Mary and me.

3

WE WERE CHILDREN in a stable world, but our adolescence, adulthood, and maturity were spent in a world that seemed to have gone mad. Yet despite the colossal dislocations of the Great Depression, World War II, and the Cold War, we have managed to go along living our lives, developing our marriage, and rearing our family in comparative serenity.

After I had given Mary the engagement ring and we had selected the date for the wedding, I began to save money in earnest. I had never before saved it at all. I remember that I was obscurely disgusted in boyhood with my brother because he had forty dollars in the bank, and I had nothing. I disdained, too, his careful practice of hanging up his clothing at night, keeping it brushed and pressed, and all that sort of thing.

Now that I was facing the responsibilities of marriage, however, I could see my brother's point. I husbanded my salary as well as I, with my temperament, was able. I was seen less often playing billiards, a game which to this day I consider the prince of them all.

We were to marry in July; and by the time that month arrived, I had $247 in the bank.

But I had not saved this royal sum for the sake of saving it, but for the sake of spending it. I made a down payment

18

on a four-cylinder Ford. I do not remember whether I bought a new suit, although I suppose that I did. I set aside a stipend for the priest and a gift for the altar boys, and found myself in possession of $70 for the honeymoon.

Mary and I were determined upon one thing: we would not live with relatives — or for that matter with anybody else. In preparation for our marriage, we rented a three-room apartment for $30 a month. It was situated on what we promptly dubbed the Boulevard of the Alleys — a take-off on the Boulevard of the Allies in Pittsburgh.

The apartment was on one of two narrow streets with a little strip of park between them, where we thought the children (we were already dreaming of children) could play. As it turned out, we lived on the Boulevard of the Alleys three months.

I obtained, on credit, a davenport and chair, and some kitchen furniture. Mary already owned iron twin beds, complete with springs and mattresses. Her mother and mine donated bedclothing, knives and forks, cooking utensils, dishes and the like.

We moved our few possessions into the little apartment, arranged and rearranged them, and stood back for a moment surveying our first home. We kissed each other ceremoniously, went outside, and locked the front door. I dropped the key into my pocket with a feeling of immense importance, and handed Mary into the Ford.

We were ready to speak our vows, to come together as husband and wife, and to establish one of those little nations, those little worlds, which are called families.

We were early for our wedding, and yet we were late. This bit of time-space magic was made possible by Mary's mercurial nephew, Dick. Dick and his brother Fred were altar boys for our nuptial Mass. Among their duties was that of keeping watch for our arrival, and heralding our approach by seizing a big rope and ringing the bell of our parish church.

This was not the little wooden church in which we had been baptized and learned the catechism. It was a towering new church, and its great bell could be heard over much of the town.

Mary and I were to ride to church in her brother Ralph's new and shining Chevrolet. Unfortunately, Dick and Fred had not been warned that Ralph might drive somebody else to church before he brought us. Fifteen or twenty minutes before we were due, Dick saw the Chevrolet approaching, and instantly set the bell to clamoring.

Mary and I heard the sound at her mother's house, where we were waiting. We surmised what had happened. The moment Ralph returned, we jumped hastily into his car and hurried to the church.

We had been carefully coached not to walk up the aisle until the organist finished her introduction to the wedding march, but we broke the rule when we saw white-haired Father Edgar standing patiently at the altar, to which he had gone upon hearing the bell. We arrived at the altar before the organ introduction was half finished.

"Marriage," says the Church in its instructions for those entering upon that state of life, "is a sacrament instituted by Jesus Christ in order to unite, by an indissoluble bond, two souls whom God has made for each other, and who will love and be devoted to each other, as Christ also loved the Church and delivered Himself up for it."

Such is the high and noble romance of the Christian truth

about marriage. But I suppose that Mary and I are by no means the only couple who little appreciated, until much later, the splendor of the life upon which we were entering.

I am sure that we hardly heard, standing there at the altar, the magnificent blessings which our venerable pastor, Father Edgar, was calling down upon us in a voice beginning to quaver with age.

Bless, O Lord, this union, and from heaven watch over it. . . .

Deign, O Lord, to send upon this man and wife Thy blessing; that they may continue in Thy favor, persevere in Thy will, and abide in Thy love. Through Christ Our Lord.

Thus prayed Father Edgar in the glorious ancient prose of the Church, lifting his blue-veined old hand in the Sign of the Cross above our bowed heads.

May the Lord God Almighty bless you with the fulness of His benediction; may you see your children's children even to the third and fourth generation, and may you attain to a happy old age. Through Christ Our Lord.

May the God of Israel join you together; and may He be with you. . . .

The aged voice murmured the noble benedictions; but we were too young and too thoughtless, we had not lived enough and suffered enough, to appreciate them as they deserved. We were like children as we stood there entering upon a union so important for future generations that it might well have struck angels with awe.

And now, O Lord, make them bless Thee more fully. . . .
Thy wife shall be as a fruitful vine on the sides of thy house. Thy children as olive-plants round about thy table.

The divine poetry, the great benedictions, descended upon us; but we did not really hear them. We were not ready to attend to them, to realize their beauty, until years later, when we were older and much wiser.

Father Edgar lifted his voice and hands in the final blessing:

May the God of Abraham, the God of Isaac, and the God of Jacob be with you, and may He fulfill His blessing in you: that you may see your children's children even to the third and fourth generation, and thereafter may you have life everlasting, by the grace of Our Lord Jesus Christ.

It was ended. The organ burst forth in a joyful paean. Mary and I rose from our knees and fled from the church; fled along the aisle between the stained-glass windows into the bright sunshine outside. There was only one thing in the marriage service that we had truly understood and profoundly encompassed with our minds and wills:

I take thee to have and to hold from this day forward; for better, for worse, for richer, for poorer, in sickness and in health, until death do us part, and thereto I plight thee my troth.

That much we had really grasped; and it was enough to carry us onward and upward toward the time when we should grasp the other great truths that had been uttered to us.

We fled from the church, and we did not yet comprehend the splendid Christian facts about marriage.

Two souls whom God has made for each other. . .

Thus speaks the Church; but I wonder whether one in a hundred of the young men and women who approach the altar together ever appreciate the magnificence of the vocation into which they are entering.

Joe and Mary who had just administered the Sacrament of Matrimony to each other fled down the steps of the church, piled into Ralph's Chevrolet, and rode away through the July heat, between the little houses and under the trees arching above the winding streets.

I had conferred upon Mary, and she upon me, one of the Seven Sacraments instituted by the Redeemer to make men and women holy. We had called down from heaven the goodness of God upon each other. But we did not know. We did not realize. We thought we were merely Joe and Mary.

We ran up the wooden steps of Mary's home, and into the tiny parlor. There we stood, looking at each other as if we had never before met. We stood there waiting awkwardly for the relatives to arrive, and I do not think that I so much as kissed Mary. We had not appreciated the great blessings and the great poetry, but one thing we did understand — we were husband and wife; and the realization overwhelmed us. It made us suddenly shy.

Soon the relatives came flocking in, effusive with congratulations. Out of the corner of my eye, I saw Mary startle my father's enormous humility into blushes by suddenly and unexpectedly kissing him as he held out his hand to her.

Mary kissed my father, and I shook hands, awkwardly and embarrassedly, with her father and mother.

Mary and I were strangely unhungry. All through the wedding breakfast, we sat nibbling, occasionally letting our eyes meet each other's for a moment, and smiling mechanically at the chaffing of relatives.

Mary's mother again demonstrated her great good sense.

As soon as she could, she announced that Mary and I had a long trip ahead of us (it wasn't really long) and ought to get started. We smiled gratefully at her.

In a few minutes, we were running out to the Ford amid a small shower of rice. I opened the door for Mary, got in behind the wheel, stepped on the starter, and waited impatiently for the last good-byes to be uttered.

I was about to let out the clutch and chug away when Mary's mother approached and handed through the open window a cardboard box. "That's a little snack for you, in case you get hungry," she said with a motherly smile.

Hunger was the last thing I expected, but I thanked her — I am afraid a bit perfunctorily — tossed the box into the back seat, slid the car into gear, and we were off.

Within twenty minutes we were out in the country on the other side of the Kiskiminetas River, tooling along a hot ribbon of highway under a blazing July sun.

I looked ahead and saw nothing. I looked to right and left and there were no houses. I glanced in my rear-view mirror; the road behind us was empty.

I stopped the car and leaned toward Mary, sliding my arm around her shoulders.

"Joe. Someone might see."

"No. We're all alone."

She yielded, and I kissed her.

Instantly there was a great hooting from an automobile horn, and a carload of workmen swept past, shouting.

"Joe!" exclaimed Mary, reproachfully.

"I'd have sworn there was nobody near us," I said. Blushing and grinning, I put the car into gear again, and we resumed our honeymoon journey.

From that time on, as we wound through the Pennsylvania hills, anyone seeing us might have thought we were barely acquainted. I stayed on my side of the car, and Mary on hers.

I think we could hardly have covered more than fifteen miles when I became conscious of hunger. I stopped the car, pulled off the road, reached back a long arm for the box Mary's mother had handed me, and opened it. It was filled with chicken sandwiches.

"Hungry?" I asked Mary.

She took a sandwich. I took one. Then we took another. By the time our appetites were satisfied, the box was empty. And I doubt that any wedding breakfast has ever tasted better than that one, eaten along the roadside under the flaming sun, while a herd of cows in a neighboring field grazed contentedly.

Two souls whom God has made for each other . . .

The Sacrament of Matrimony is a communion of life, physical, intellectual and moral.

We ate our sandwiches in innocent ignorance of the gigantic importance of a husband and wife in the eyes of the Church. Years later, I was to read with profound appreciation an ancient Christian formula for the marriage vow:

"With this ring I thee wed; this gold and silver I thee give; with my body I thee worship; and with all my worldly goods I thee endow."

We sat there eating our sandwiches, unconscious of the immensity of the divine and human seas, the natural and supernatural oceans, upon which we had set sail together.

May you see your children's children . . .

So prays the Church.

We nearly failed to see even our children. As we drove into the outskirts of the town where we intended to spend our honeymoon, an automobile swerved across the road and smashed into our little Ford, tearing and crumpling our fenders, crushing the running board, bending the doors and wheels, and flinging our car against the curbing.

The sounds of crashing, crumpling, and scraping stopped. There was a moment of stunned silence. Then, simultaneously, "Are you all right, Mary?" I asked, and "Are you all right, Joe?" she inquired.

We were.

I got out and stood looking at our smashed car.

A little knot of bystanders was gathering around us, murmuring sympathetically.

Someone volunteered the information that there was a Ford agency nearby. Mary and I walked there and told the manager our troubles. He sent out a tow truck, brought the car in, examined it, and assured us that it could be repaired within a few days. We took a bus to the hotel where we were to stay, hard by the shores of Lake Conneaut.

For the first time, I signed the words "Mr. and Mrs. Joseph A. Breig." A bellhop took our luggage, led us to our room, accepted a tip, and left us.

The sun had turned the world into a furnace. The humid air was like a steaming blanket flung around us. The hotel room was, if anything, hotter than the flaming outdoors.

Mary took off her hat. I took off my coat. We sat and stared at each other. "My car," I said. "My new car, smashed."

"They'll fix it, Joe."

"But it won't be new any more. And I wanted it to be new for our honeymoon."

"The man said he'd fix it as good as new."

I mopped at my steaming face with a handkerchief. "I'm going to wash."

As I flung back my arms to slip out of my shirt, I felt pain. "Is there something wrong with my back?"

Mary looked. My back was streaked with welts and brush burns. Apparently I had been flung against the door when the automobile smashed into ours.

While Mary was applying a cold wet towel to my back, I thought of something. "It's a good thing I wasn't driving with my elbow out the window. I might be minus one arm."

She touched my arm. "Don't *ever* drive with your elbow out the window."

We sat down limply, crushed by the heat. Mary sniffed. "Do you smell cooking?"

I did. I went to the window and looked down. The clerk had given us a room directly above the kitchen, where the heat of the stoves compounded the boiling heat of the day.

"It's because we're here on a due bill from the newspaper," I grumbled. "If we were paying cash, they wouldn't dare offer us a room like this."

Mary smiled. "If it weren't for the due bill, we couldn't have come at all. We'd have had to spend our honeymoon at home."

"Fine way to start our married life," I growled. "An auto wreck and a room over the kitchen. We can't even go for a ride to get cool."

She took my hand. "Never mind. It's all right."

Two days later, we went back to the automobile agency, and were shown our car. We could hardly believe our eyes. It looked as if it had come, that very moment, out of the factory.

I went into the manager's office. "Your mechanics did a wonderful job."

He thanked me.

"How much?" I asked.

He slid a statement across his desk.

Sixty dollars.

I took all the money I had out of my pocket and showed it to him. "Sixty-five dollars," I said. "Just enough to pay you and buy gasoline to go home. I wouldn't mind that, but this is the third day of my honeymoon."

The manager looked startled. "Honeymoon?"

I nodded. He turned and looked through the glass wall of his office at Mary, who was waiting in the showroom. The light coming through the big front windows made a cameo of her face.

The manager looked back at me, his eyes sympathetic.

"Can you identify yourself?"

I produced my driver's and owner's licenses for the car, my newspaperman's pass. He glanced at them and handed them back. He drew a paper from his desk drawer, filled it out, and slid it across the desk. "It's a note for sixty dollars," he said. "Sign it, and pay me when you can. I'll not interfere with any man's honeymoon."

I signed, shook hands, parted from him, and led Mary to our rejuvenated Ford. I drove gaily toward the hotel.

"You'd never know the car had been so much as scratched," I remarked happily to Mary.

She touched my hand, sympathizing. She understood how proud I was of my first new automobile.

After a moment, she inquired, "Did you pay for the repairs, Joe? Do we have to go home?"

I told her what the manager had done. She smiled happily.

The heat had not abated. The motion of the car did little to relieve our discomfort. The breezes that came in through the windows were hot and humid. The sun glared blindingly.

We parked the car at the hotel and went to our sultry room above the kitchen. I decided that we had endured enough. "Let's go somewhere else," I suggested.

"Where?"

"Our due bill is good for a hotel in Washington."

"But won't Washington be terribly hot?"

"It can't be hotter than this," I said. "At least, we won't be right over the kitchen. And there are things to see in Washington. Have you ever been there?"

"No."

"You'd enjoy the Lincoln Memorial, the Washington Monument—all those things."

Mary fanned her face with her hand. "I'm willing. I'd rather be riding than sitting here."

Thirty minutes later we were tooling along through the Pennsylvania hills again, southward toward our nation's capital; toward the White House and Capitol Hill and Mount Vernon, where lay buried a man who had left that splendid mansion to suffer in the snows of Valley Forge for . . . well, for us and for our children and our children's children, even unto the third and fourth generation.

4

Our honeymoon arrival in the capital of our country was uneventful. No parade along Constitution Avenue welcomed us. No diplomats in top hats received us. The President did not emerge from the White House to shake hands.

There was no official recognition of the fact that to Washington had come an ambassador and an ambassadress representing earth's most venerable institution — marriage — and that their credentials bore the seal of divine approval and of all the experience of humankind back to the dawn of time.

Nevertheless, Washington did welcome us unofficially, if not officially. Washington did recognize our importance, in the vague and kindly way in which the world continues to reverence romance and marriage. The national capital did lay down for us, in an informal and popular fashion, a red carpet.

Washington received us as we had been received a few weeks earlier in Greensburg, the seat of our Westmoreland County in Pennsylvania, when we went there to obtain our marriage license. As we entered the courthouse between the stately columns, we were welcomed by a venerable official functionary in a uniform. He did not ask our business; he bowed with a great smile and said, "Right this way. Just follow me." And he led us with happy ceremoniousness to the Marriage License Bureau, for all the world as if we had been distinguished visitors.

It was like that in the national capital, too. Taximen and newsboys and bystanders conspired to direct us to our hotel; and their cheery kindliness was better than a twenty-one gun salute.

When we walked into the Capitol building, we were greeted by guides as if we were potentates from some friendly power. As we toiled up the last of the steps into the Lincoln Memorial, we were taken in tow and led before the great statue of the Emancipator, where we stood in awe for a time before turning to read the Gettysburg Address chiseled into the stone wall.

We did not meet the President, but we were escorted through parts of the White House by smiling guides who seemed able to recognize a honeymooning couple at a glance.

Even the hotel clerk seemed to be part of the conspiracy of hospitality. He looked at our due bill from the *Vandergrift News,* and assigned us not to a room, but to a suite, complete with living room. Not even the high ceilings and the stone walls could keep out the blazing July heat, but at least we did not stifle, as we had in the little room above the kitchen in the first hotel.

Our Mount Vernon visit turned out to be more of an adventure than we expected. Soon after we started back to Washington, Mary became ill.

The pallor of her face alarmed me. We were going through a little town, and I stopped and inquired for a physician. We drew up in front of a white colonial house with tall pillars supporting a high porch.

Inside, a kindly doctor examined Mary, ordered a colored

servant to bring a lemonade for her, prescribed some medicine, and instructed me to keep her out of the sun and bathe her forehead with cold towels.

"She's got a touch of sunstroke," he said. "You know, young man, she's not as strong as you are. And a honeymoon can be a bit of a strain."

Mary recovered quickly. Next day she said she was well enough to go to Baltimore to visit my Aunt Kate and Aunt Tillie. We would not dare go home to Vandergrift and admit to my mother that we had been within forty miles of her sisters, and had not seen them.

The Ford sped us along the shimmering highway to Baltimore. We threaded through traffic to Penrose Avenue, where identical brick apartments stood in bewildering connected rows, each apartment brave with its four or five stone steps, washed and polished to a gleaming whiteness.

We gathered that, in Baltimore, white steps are required for any kind of social standing, and a footprint on one of them is a kind of sacrilege.

Our car moved slowly along the street while Mary and I peered at house numbers. Then I put on the brake, touched Mary's hand, and pointed ahead through the windshield.

I had spied Aunt Kate. For all her eighty years, she was kneeling, her back to us, on her white marble steps, finishing her daily cleansing of them.

We watched for a moment, then stared at each other in amazement. Aunt Kate, we knew, had recently emerged from a hospital. She had been struck down by an automobile in a driving rain while crossing a street, almost invisible under an enormous black umbrella. At first, the surgeon had simply ordered the nurses to make her as comfortable as possible. It was taken for granted that she would not survive.

The surgeon did not know Aunt Kate! He did not know that she was one of the most indomitable women who ever lived — or decided to go on living. When he realized that he was dealing with one who had not the faintest intention of dying, he patched together the fractured hip, prescribed crutches and a special shoe with a heel raised a couple of inches, and sent Aunt Kate home with orders to stay in the house.

Aunt Kate snorted, fitted the crutches under her armpits, and resumed her normal routine of haggling with hucksters, "redding up" the house, scouring the front steps each day with soap and stone, and simultaneously bullying and protecting her gentle sister Aunt Tillie.

While we watched through the windshield on that broiling July day, Aunt Kate gave the steps a final swipe, and dropped her polishing stone and soap into a bucket of water, which she lifted to the stoop at the front door. She squeezed the water out of her scrubbing cloth, raised her hand, and allowed the cloth to unfold.

Mary and I gasped. The cloth must have been nearly two yards in length. Reaching across from the side of the steps, Aunt Kate arranged it so that it formed a kind of carpet up to the door. Then, walking on hands and feet, and lifting her shortened leg with a stiff crablike motion, she made her way up the steps without touching foot to their immaculate surfaces.

Reaching the door, she put the bucket inside, turned, backed herself into a chair in the doorway, hauled in her long cloth hand over hand, dropped it in the bucket, and raised herself to her crutches, which were leaning within arm's reach. In a moment, she had dragged bucket and chair out of sight. The front door slammed, and she was gone.

Mary and I woke from the spell. We looked at each other and smiled; but we did not laugh. Young though we were, and unacquainted with pain and infirmity, we realized something of the simple and unconscious heroism in the scene we had watched. We had beheld a kind of capsuled demonstration of the industry and independence, the self-reliance and good pride, which were part of the secret of our country, from whose capital we had just come.

I slid the car into gear and moved it slowly to a stop in front of the unpretentious little home into which Aunt Kate had vanished. Mary and I got out and stood in the hot sun, looking at the gleaming steps.

"How are we going to get up there," I asked, pointing toward the front door, "without soiling those steps?"

"Well, we can't fly," said Mary. She took my arm. "We'll just have to walk on them."

We went on tiptoe to the front door. I pushed a button set into the woodwork, and was startled to hear a deafening clamor from an electric gong. After a moment, I chuckled.

"Aunt Kate is a bit hard of hearing," I told Mary. "And Aunt Tillie is worse."

Answering the doorbell was a privilege which Aunt Kate had virtually monopolized for sixty years, ever since the day she and Aunt Tillie, young women fresh from the family farm in Somerset County, Pennsylvania, had set up housekeeping together in Baltimore.

She opened the door now, peered out at us, and cried "Well?" in a high-pitched, cracked voice, plentifully touched

with the astringency which comes of fighting life out, toe to
toe, against the difficulties and obstacles of a big city.

I stood grinning, towering above her. "Don't you know
me, Aunt Kate?"

Her fearless old eyes rose to mine and her voice soared
to its highest register. She thumped one of her crutches on
the wooden floor. "Tillie! Till! It's the honeymooners! It's Joe
and his bride!" And she turned and lolloped, crutch and
shoe, shoe and crutch, away from us along the narrow hall
toward the kitchen, shrilling her sister's name.

I followed, drawing Mary after me. We came into the
kitchen to see Aunt Tillie, her face wearing a bewildered
expression, cupping her hand behind her ear while Aunt
Kate cried at her, "The honeymooners!"

"What money?" Aunt Tillie was asking.

Just then she saw us and scrambled to her feet, saying
softly and prayerfully, "Bless my soul, bless my soul."

While Mary and I kissed the withered old cheek, Aunt
Tillie was saying reproachfully, "Kate, where's your manners?
You didn't even invite them to come in." But there was an
undertone of affectionate laughter in her voice.

Aunt Kate bristled. She almost always bristled, no matter
what Aunt Tillie said. "Since when do Joe and his wife
need an invitation?" she demanded.

Aunt Tillie was holding Mary at arm's length, inspecting
her. "Why, Kate," she was saying, "she's beautiful. Isn't she
beautiful? Who would ever have thought that a beautiful
girl like this would marry our Joe?"

But Aunt Kate was intent upon settling the other issue.
"Since when do Joe and his wife need an invitation?" she
repeated.

Often, from earliest childhood, I had heard my mother remarking humorously that her two Baltimore sisters fought like Kilkenny cats, but couldn't bear to be apart. I didn't know what Kilkenny cats were, or how they fought, but I thought it wise to distract Aunt Kate from the argument.

"Got anything to eat?" I inquired.

"Bless my soul," cried Aunt Tillie in her quavering voice. "Kate, they're hungry. Where's your manners?"

Aunt Kate thumped a crutch on the floor and said, as if she had not heard — as perhaps she hadn't — "Till, didn't you hear what Joe said? They're hungry — and you stand around mooning about how beautiful the bride is."

And she bustled into the tiny kitchen, grumbling, "Of course she's beautiful, but she can't eat compliments."

Aunt Kate and Aunt Tillie were the Martha and the Mary of my mother's family, the McKenzies. The McKenzies were a numerous brood, reared on a then-remote farm near the Mason-Dixon Line which marks the Pennsylvania-Maryland border. They were descended from a Scottish Highlander Catholic family which settled in America before the Revolution; and there was a tradition that seven McKenzie brothers had fought with General Washington for independence.

Being Scots, the McKenzies had a reputation for thrift, but my mother had often told me laughingly that a good German hausfrau could rear a family comfortably in circumstances in which most Scots would starve.

However that may be, Aunt Kate and Aunt Tillie had survived in Baltimore only by "making do" with very little. Yet their thrift, which was almost incredible, had not the faintest touch of closefistedness. They were, in fact, extraordinarily generous.

These two spinsters, who had always seemed to me ancient because they were older than my mother, had poured themselves out in many ways for my sisters and brother and me. They never came to visit us without bringing presents, and now and then they sent to each of us a hard-earned half dollar or dollar.

Aunt Kate's loan of something like five hundred dollars, painstakingly saved in dimes and quarters, had helped to establish my father in business. Aunt Tillie we regarded as a saint, and we knew that she had adopted, spiritually, each of us as we came into the world, and thereafter, like a remote guardian angel, watched over us with her prayers.

"You'll have a lot of thanking of Aunt Tillie to do, you scalawags, if you ever get to heaven," my mother often told us. And it is a simple fact that sometimes in the years after her death, when I was desperate for rest because of a squalling infant, I saw the little one go peacefully to sleep after I had uttered a little prayer for Aunt Tillie's intercession in heaven.

Aunt Kate, too, was an exceedingly good woman, in her Martha-ish and Kilkenny-cat sort of way. We always thought of her as entertaining in her faults — lovable in spite of them, and admirable for one enormous virtue — a courage that would have bearded the devil in hell in defense of one of her loved ones. When we were with Aunt Tillie, we felt protective toward her; but when we were with Aunt Kate, we felt protected, as if surrounded by an army of ferociously loyal retainers.

"Till! Don't stand there gabbling," shrilled Aunt Kate now in the voice that seemed always raised to its highest register. We could hear the clumping of her crutches in the little kitchen. "Stop gabbling and come help get something to eat for Joe and Mary. Can't you see they're starving?"

Soon the two of them were pottering about, arguing companionably in their old voices, while Mary and I took turns washing in a bathroom no larger than the average wardrobe.

While we ate a snack, they plied us with questions. Aunt Kate wanted to know about everybody at home, and Aunt Tillie wanted to know about us. Her angelic little face beamed, and her old eyes, beginning now to grow dim, glowed as she shared vicariously in our honeymoon.

Aunt Tillie was as romantic as a schoolgirl; Aunt Kate considered romance what she called "stuff and nonsense" — or so she pretended. Nevertheless, she listened to every word as I answered Aunt Tillie's questions about how Mary and I had met, and about the wedding.

Mary washed the dishes and I dried them, using salt sacks which Aunt Kate had thriftily saved and sewed together. They were about as absorbent as leather, and I found it impossible to get the dishes more than theoretically dry. Mary made a mental note about it, and sent a dozen tea towels after we returned home.

Years later, after the two aunts had died, the towels were found packed neatly away, and were part of their little legacy to us.

After we finished the dishes, I left Mary chatting with my aunts, and sauntered through the narrow hall and down the sacrosanct steps into the blazing sunlight. The woman next door was standing at her door.

"Hello," she said. "Are you the nephew that just got married?"

I admitted it.

She looked to make sure that I had closed the Aunt Kate-Aunt Tillie door. "Those aunts of yours," she observed, "are a couple of characters."

"That's a mighty big understatement," I told her.

"They're getting old," she went on. "They need someone to look after them."

This time, it was I who looked to see whether the door was closed. I could imagine Aunt Kate's towering wrath if she should ever hear anybody suggest that she was incapable of taking care of herself — and of everybody else.

I grinned at the woman next door. "My mother has been trying for years to get those two to come live with us. Not a chance. They did come once, intending to stay. They lasted two weeks. Then they were homesick for Baltimore, and they packed up and came back here."

The woman sighed. "I suppose when you've lived sixty years in a place — ." She laughed. "You know, I think everybody in Baltimore knows Aunt Kate."

And she began to reminisce, as people often did when Aunt Kate was mentioned.

The woman recalled that Aunt Kate no sooner got home from the hospital, after her automobile accident, than she began to disobey the doctor.

"The doctor told her to stay indoors, and not to go up or down stairs. The very next morning, she propped her crutches outside the door, came down the steps sitting down, like a small child, reached up, got her crutches, and hobbled to the bank. The manager gave her a good scolding and brought her home in his automobile.

"Come Saturday evening, she crutched her way to church and went to confession. The priest left the confessional and

brought her home. He scolded her too, and said that any
time she wanted to confess, he'd come to the house. Aunt
Kate told him he'd do nothing of the kind. 'I'll confess
through the screen, where you can't see me, young man,'
she said.

"Then the policeman on this beat came to see her, and
he scolded her, too. But she got up on her crutches and
shooed him to the door, telling him that Baltimore would
be a better city if the police department would spend more
time catching burglars, and less time interfering with the
affairs of law-abiding, taxpaying citizens."

The woman paused, smiling, and asked, "Can't *you* give
her a good talking-to?"

I stared at her incredulously. She was not joking. I pointed
eloquently at my chest. "*Me?* Why, she used to change my
diapers. She thinks I haven't sense enough to come in out
of the rain."

Just then the front door was yanked open and Aunt Kate
stood there, pointing a crutch at me. "Joe!" she shrilled.
"Come in out of that sun this very instant, before you get
sunstroke. Haven't you an ounce of brains?"

I shrugged at the woman next door, and spread my
hands apart. She chuckled. "I see what you mean," she
said. She watched, smiling, while I tiptoed up the immaculate steps and into the comparative coolness of the
dim hall.

I half-expected Aunt Kate to take me by the ear, but
she didn't. I am quite certain that this was not because
she recognized my new dignity as a married man. I think
it was because I had grown so tall that she couldn't reach
my ear without dropping a crutch and losing her balance.

Mary and I slept that night on a sofa which opened to form a bed in the little parlor. I remonstrated with Aunt Kate and Aunt Tillie when I realized that they were still sleeping on the second floor, which was reached by a murderously steep and narrow flight of steps. I said, "Why don't you make a bedroom out of this parlor, and stay downstairs?"

Aunt Kate looked at me as if I had gone stark mad. I gave up.

In the world of Aunt Kate and Aunt Tillie, a woman might get along without food, but she certainly would not get along without a parlor which she could keep always in perfect order against the advent of visitors.

At bedtime, Aunt Kate scornfully brushed aside my offer to help her up the stairs. "How do you suppose I get along when you're not here?" she snorted.

I couldn't imagine how she did, and I watched curiously to find out. First, she laid her crutches slantwise on the steps, and tied a string to them. Then she sat down on the second step and went up backward, sitting on each step in turn.

At the top of the stairway, a chair was waiting for her. She worked herself up into it, and then pulled the string, hand over hand, until the crutches reached her. She detached the string, got the crutches under her armpits, stood up, said good night, and vanished.

"Good night," I told her, and went into the parlor, shaking my head.

Mary and I were awakened next morning by a frightful clatter. We sat up in bed, staring at each other. "O Lord," I groaned, "Aunt Kate has fallen downstairs."

I jumped out of bed and ran to the stairway. The

crutches were lying helter-skelter in the hallway. I looked up the steps, holding my breath. Aunt Kate was coming down, step by step, on her bottom.

"Good morning," she said. "Up kind of early aren't you?"

"Aunt Kate," I asked, "why don't you let the crutches down quietly by the string, instead of throwing them down the steps?"

"That's too slow," she said; and reaching the bottom, she gathered her crutches to her, stood up, and was ready for another day.

It was still blazing hot — although it was late evening — when we said good-by to the aunts, kissed them, turned away from the tears in their eyes, and drove back to Washington.

We reached the city before midnight, got lost in the traffic circles, and did not reach our hotel until two o'clock in the morning. Again we made a sudden decision.

"Let's get out of here," I said as we reached our sweltering room. "It's too hot."

The night clerk looked startled as we approached, carrying suitcases. "Anything wrong?" he asked anxiously. "Too hot," I told him. He did not dispute the statement.

A bellboy helped us outside with our bags, and watched while we started the car and drove away.

√   We stopped at a couple of service stations, because my gasoline supply was low; but they were closed. Presently an automobile pulled up beside us at a traffic light. A man leaned out the window and said in a soft southern voice, "I beg your pardon, suh, but I am a police officer, and I saw you stopping in gasoline stations. Is there something I can do for you?"

I was speechless. I had never heard a policeman talk

like that. I managed to stammer that we needed gasoline, and were trying to find the highway that led north into Pennsylvania.

"Follow me, if you please, suh," said this extraordinary officer. He led us to an all-night station, waited until we got our tank filled, and then conducted us to the highway.

I tried to thank him. "Not at all, suh; this is my duty," he said, and was gone, leaving a memory which amazes us to this day.

We drove until we were in our familiar Pennsylvania mountains. It was cool there. For the first time since we had started on our honeymoon, we were out of the suffocating heat.

I pulled the car off the road into a pasture, laid Mary's coat across her in the back seat, curled up in the front seat, and went to sleep.

When we woke, refreshed, the sun was high in the heavens, and cows were grazing peaceably all around the Ford. We smiled at each other. "The best hotel we've been in," I said to Mary, "and it was free!"

5

WITHIN THE FIRST YEAR of our marriage, we moved three times. "Flittings," my mother-in-law called these transfers from house to house.

She was an old hand at the process. Often she had found it necessary to "flit" from steel town to steel town so that her husband might find employment amid the fluctuations of industry. From her, Mary had learned facility in packing and unpacking. I made a few bungling attempts to help, but soon enough Mary suggested that I leave the movings to her.

It gave me an odd, unrealistic feeling to get up in the morning in one house, go to work, and come home for lunch in another house. But I had no objections to the flittings, as long as they contributed to Mary's happiness. Knowing my absent-mindedness, she telephoned before lunch each time to remind me that we had moved.

Our reason for leaving our first little honeymoon apartment was simple. It was too small. We moved with high hopes into a five-room place, but began to have misgivings the very day we arrived, because of something that happened while the moving men were carrying in furniture. The landlady came out of her big house on the front of the lot and commanded the men to follow her. Two men and a teen-age boy meekly obeyed. They descended into the basement, and presently the two men emerged, empty-handed and wearing broad derisive grins. Behind them came the boy, carrying in his arms what must surely have been the smallest coal stove ever made. This, we discovered with something like horror, was our heating system.

We had inspected the apartment in late summer, and had assumed, innocently, that some kind of modern and adequate stove would be installed with the approach of cold weather. We soon enough discovered that not even the most ingenious Boy Scout could have kept a blaze going through the night in the peanut shell of a stove the boy had carried in.

Each morning, Mary and I awakened to find the house as cold as an abandoned igloo. Often the walls were damp with condensed moisture. I would leap out of bed shuddering in the chill air, cram paper and wood into the tiny stove, place two or three lumps of coal carefully on top of the kindling, touch a flame to the paper, and jump back into bed. But the first tentative blaze made only a token impression on the tomblike cold of the place, and in the end I had to venture forth from the covers again and dash into my clothing, shivering. Hours would pass before the rooms were approximately warm.

But the place had an even worse fault. The man in the apartment below worked the evening shift in the steel mill, and arrived home each night thirty minutes after midnight, his eardrums apparently calloused with the clamor and thunder of the open hearth. For him, 12:30 a.m. was evening; it was supper time. Invariably, he turned on his radio

as loud as possible and tuned to a station broadcasting hill-
billy music. This would go on for hours, while Mary and
I tossed and turned, trying uselessly to sleep.

One night I told Mary, grinding my teeth, "I'll fix that
guy." I got out of bed and detached the iron trimmings from
our little stove. Then, for ten or fifteen minutes, I worked
off my anger by banging them together, throwing them with
a clang and a clatter to the floor, picking them up, and
throwing them again.

Mary sat up in bed watching me with that puzzled expression which always comes into her face when anybody
exhibits temper. "It won't do any good, Joe," she assured me.

She was right. The hideous uproar from the radio downstairs continued. Apparently our neighbors were blissfully
unconscious of the fact that the racket upstairs was intended
as a hint to them.

Eventually we moved to get away from the uproar and
the cold.

This time, we found an ideal place; but our enjoyment
of it was short-lived. The year was 1931, and the Great
Depression was slowing American industry nearly to a stand-
still. Each month, the payrolls in the steel plant grew smaller.
More and more men were becoming jobless. Business fell off
catastrophically in my father's store, where I had first met
Mary.

One day in early summer, when the flowers Mary had
planted were thrusting forth their green magic, I came
home to tell her glumly that in order to help my father to
try to keep his financial head above water, we would have to
move into one of the little flats above his store. He needed
the rent desperately, and had been unable to find a tenant.

It was a bitter blow for Mary, but she took it like the valiant young woman she was. We flitted to the flat.

There, in the place where I had spent my childhood and adolescence, our first son was born some months later, and immediately died. There we lived through the blackest times of the Depression, while my father went into bankruptcy, and my salary as a newspaperman grew smaller and smaller. It was a strange, depressing period, but we learned much from it that was valuable.

For me, the flat was thronged with memories. Here I had lived from earliest childhood. Here, when I misbehaved, I had been thrust into a dark closet that we called the Spook Hole. To this day I heartily disapprove of such methods of discipline.

Here I had browsed through a little treasury of books, stored in a great tall bookcase with glass doors, which I once upset while climbing the shelves to get at a book beyond my reach. Fortunately, I was not injured, because the hall was so narrow that the bookcase was checked in its fall by the wall opposite.

Here, in the kitchen, I had watched my mother making "potato water," kneading dough, and baking bread which came out of the oven brown and appetizing. Here I had turned the wringer on the old hand-operated washing machine, while Mother guided the dripping wash through the rollers.

Here was the dining room where the family life had centered. Here we had studied our school lessons. Here was the coal stove around which we had huddled to dress on winter mornings after jumping out of bed in cold bedrooms. Here my brother and I had conducted our chemical experiments, once making the entire flat uninhabitable for hours by filling it with the fumes of burning sulphur.

Here I can still see my father towering above us, bellowing with relieved laughter in his deep voice, because nothing worse had happened than that we had ruined the dining-room carpet by upsetting a bucket of paint on it.

Mother had run down the back steps to the store, almost hysterical, crying, "George! The boys —. The boys —." That was all she was able to gasp out. Father came up the steps three at a time, his head filled with harrowing visions of burned or scalded or bleeding children.

He was so happy to see us unhurt that he refused to dole out even token punishment, and it was years before my mother really forgave him for his laughter. To Mother, a carpet was something immensely important; to Father, it was nothing. You could buy a new carpet, but you could not buy new sons and daughters.

It was a marvel, though, that my brother and I ever lived beyond boyhood. From our high back porch, a flight of steps led to a wooden structure on the roof, which we called The Cabin. There we conducted all kinds of experiments, which seem dangerous in retrospect, with Bunsen burners, electricity, and chemicals.

I remember that once we stood on the edge of the roof with our friend Herb Brown, looking down on the street forty feet below, vieing with one another to see which of us could extend his toes farthest into empty space without toppling over.

The back porch was supported by long steel poles, up and down which we shinnied like monkeys. Why nobody ever fell off, I cannot imagine, although we did have some little judgment of what was possible, and what impossible. I recall that we often talked about trying the trick of reaching up to the porch floor, getting a grip with our fingers, letting go the pole with our legs, dangling in space for a moment, and then lifting ourselves by sheer strength of arm muscles until we could grasp the porch rail and clamber over it. We talked about that often, but happily we never tried it. No one but a trained acrobat or a human fly could have accomplished it.

In the basement of Father's store he had a shop. I have often marveled at the confidence with which he showed us how to operate the machinery and handle the tools, and then left us to our own devices. We suffered some cuts and bruises, but there was never a serious injury; and certainly we learned a great deal, and developed our ingenuity by designing and making things.

Walking around in the flat after Mary and I moved there, I lived over and over again my childhood and boyhood. Under the table in this room I had built forts out of blocks with Joe Johnston, who died at the age of six and left me in a bewildering loneliness. But that was not my first experience of death.

In a bed in one of the bedrooms, my grandmother had lived out her last slow years. She was a very special friend of mine. Often, when I went into her room, she reached under her pillow and drew out a penny for me. And no matter what mischief I got into, I was safe from punishment if I could get to Grandma's bedside before any adult captured me.

She would wave away my mother or my eldest sister, put her withered hand on my shoulder, and insist that I was a good boy. She must have died when I was very young, because I remember her alive, but not dead.

It is rather the other way around in the case of my sister Bernadine, who was two years older than I. I recall her most vividly in her casket, wearing a white dress, a little gold locket, and the patent-leather shoes of which she had been so proud. I seem to remember standing there alone for a long time, with my hands on the edge of the casket, just looking down at the sweet little face.

I was only four years of age, and I did not understand. I cannot even recall that I wept. I simply stood there wondering.

Bernadine died of diphtheria in the front bedroom, from which a door opened into my little bedroom, which we all called The Alcove. At some time during her illness, one or another of the children crept into her room and kissed her.

A great dispute ensued after this was discovered. Somehow, it was decided that I was the guilty person. I insisted that I was not, and to this day I believe that it was my sister Regina, who was two years younger than I, who really kissed Bernadine.

Nevertheless, the family doctor told me he wanted to take a look at my back. I lay down on the bed, supposing that he could learn, from an examination, that I had not been exposed to contagion. The next moment, I felt the sting of a needle as he injected toxin-antitoxin.

I was furious at the indignity and the deception. I told Mother, in the doctor's presence, that if he had told me what he really wanted to do, I would have let him do it. But I made perfectly plain that I resented having been made the victim of a foul trick. And out I stalked.

In the same room where Bernadine died, my brother Robert was born not long afterward. I am sure he has never known how I had longed for him, and in my childish way prayed for his arrival. I needed him to fill the emptiness left by Bernadine's death; and I loved him greatly — although not immediately upon his birth.

I had never seen a new baby, and I expected that Bob would come into the world large enough to play with. The doctor came along the hall to me and led me into the bedroom. He stood me beside the bed and beamed at me. My mother smiled from her pillow.

I stood looking at the red, wrinkled, scrawny, oil-bathed creature that was being offered to me for a brother. My heart sank; my throat closed. I pushed my hands into my pockets and was silent for a while. Finally, out of the depths of my disappointment came my verdict: "I don't like him. He's all greasy."

The doctor must have been a child psychologist of the first order. "You don't?" he drawled. "Well, then, I guess I'll take him away and give him to somebody else."

But I didn't dislike the baby *that* much. After all, even a scrawny, oily brother is better than none. I pretended a vast offhandedness, and said grandly, "Oh, well, I guess now that he's here, we might as well let him stay."

In that same room, some twenty years later, my own son was born. He did not seem to me red or wrinkled or scrawny, but of unearthly beauty. And I would have given of my heart's blood to see him squirm and cry, and be bathed with oil. It was not to be.

The "practical nurse" who was helping the doctor came to me where I stood praying in the little parlor. I knew that something was wrong; I had heard the sound of a gentle slapping as the doctor tried to induce the first wail. I had listened with all the force of my being for that cry, and it had not come.

"I'm afraid the baby is not going to live," the nurse whispered to me.

I went swiftly into the bedroom, glanced for an instant at Mary's face framed in dark hair on the pillow, and stepped at once into the bathroom. I filled a drinking glass with water, came back, and poured the water on the forehead of my son, saying "I baptize thee Joseph Anthony, in the Name of the Father and of the Son and of the Holy Ghost." I had given him my own name.

Then I stood, my shoulders bowed, looking at the firstborn son for whom in that instant I had procured an eternity of happiness with God. After a moment, I looked up at the doctor, a man little older than I. "Mary?" I questioned.

"She'll be all right," he said. He made a little gesture toward the baby. "I'm sorry. I did my best."

"You did," I told him. "I know that. I want to thank you." My voice broke and I went out to the kitchen. I opened a window and gulped deeply the cold January air.

The nurse dressed Joseph Anthony, Jr., and laid him on a pillow in a basket in the hall. After the doctor had gone and the nurse was asleep, I stood there for a long time looking at him. It was almost as if I were looking into a mirror. He was a tiny replica of myself.

Mary's recovery was very slow. Her spirit was crushed by the loss of the baby. She seemed unable to get enough air, and I spent much of my time seated beside her bed, reading humorous stories to her and wearing my overcoat and hat because the windows were wide open.

She tried bravely to smile as I read, but it was a wan attempt. Finally I realized the futility of the reading, and thereafter sat silently at her side, holding her hand. Never again were we to be the carefree couple we had been. We realized now the utter dependence of everything upon God.

I asked Mary whether she wanted to see the baby. She shook her head. "I couldn't stand it, Joe. Is it all right if I don't?"

"Certainly it's all right." I understood.

I held the little white casket on my knees in the back seat of an auto driven by my brother as we took my son to church. I carried the casket forward along the aisle between the stained-glass windows. I stood holding it before the altar where I had placed the ring on Mary's finger.

For better, for worse, for richer, for poorer . . .

Father Edgar was waiting at the altar, as he had waited for Mary and me on a happier day. His white head was bent under the weight of years. He lifted his hands to bless the body of my son. Again I heard the aging voice in which he had called down upon Mary and me the gigantic benedictions of the Sacrament of Matrimony.

Suddenly I was comforted; suddenly I felt the years telescoping in my future, and knew that it would not really be long before we would see our son again, tall and straight and strong in eternity.

I knelt at the cemetery while the little white box was lowered into the earth. Then I went back to Mary.

6

IT WAS A DAMP NIGHT in June. The darkness was white with fog. Mary and I were in the back seat of an auto driven by the same young doctor who had delivered our first-born. We were on our way to a hospital in a city twenty miles distant. Mary's hour had come again.

Sometimes the fog was so thick that the headlights seemed to strike a white wall. The pale drifting stuff walled us in, pressing against the automobile windows. It was as if we were alone in a white world through which we floated disembodied.

The road ran in curves and hills, lifting us to unseen heights, lowering us to invisible depths, swinging us right, swinging us left. The doctor drove silently, and we rode in silence behind him. I was holding Mary's hand. Sometimes it was limp in mine, and sometimes it squeezed hard as the pains came.

We were drifting through the mist, crossing a bridge, when we saw lights in front of us, swinging, circling, describing figure eights. The doctor slowed the car to a crawl, and stopped when his headlights picked out two Pennsylvania highway patrolmen, trim and erect in their uniforms, holding flashlights.

One of the two approached. He was young and slender. I could see the fresh boyish face under the wide-brimmed hat, and the pistol in its holster on his hip.

The doctor leaned out the window of the car. "I'm a physician," he said. "I'm taking a woman to the hospital."

The patrolman did not understand at first. His flashlight flicked into the back seat, paused for an instant on me, then illumined Mary's face. "I'm a physician," the doctor was repeating. "I'm taking this woman — ."

"Oh," said the patrolman suddenly. "I beg your pardon." He stepped back, touched his hat, waved us on, and called out, "Good luck." The next morning, the newspapers said that road blocks had been thrown up around the area because of a bank robbery.

The doctor went up the hospital steps ahead of us. I helped Mary to the front door and into the empty and echoing corridor, where a nurse, on night duty, kept vigil over the telephones. As we approached, she was taking Mary's name from the doctor, and jotting it down on an official-looking card.

Soon Mary was seated in a wheel chair and was being taken along the dim corridor to an elevator. I was alone.

I assumed that I had been forgotten. After all, a husband is not important at such a moment. Presently, however, a nurse conducted me to another floor, into another dimly lit corridor. She pointed to a bench, and said, "You can wait here."

Again I was alone.

I sat down in the semidarkness. I waited what seemed a very long time. Repeatedly, I resisted the temptation to look at my wrist watch. At last I could no longer restrain myself. I peered at the watch in the dim light. Fifteen minutes had passed.

I held the watch to my ear. It was ticking. Preposterous though it seemed, I had been there only fifteen minutes.

To left and right, the corridor went away into the dusk. I could see the outlines of the doors of a few rooms. I wondered what would happen if I should tiptoe along the hall, peering right and left in search of my wife. I wondered whether Mary might hear me if I called softly. I wondered whether she might be calling for me.

I waited.

The hard wooden bench on which I sat was so placed that I faced another corridor that led to great wide entrance doors with large windows. Against those windows, the fog pressed. It was gray, ghostly, motionless, impenetrable. It blotted out the sights and sounds of the night.

I got up and opened one of the doors, and went out into the mist. I looked upward; I could see nothing. There was no moonlight, no starlight, no reflection of sky or drifting clouds.

No breezes whispered; no night birds called; no crickets shrilled; no trees rustled. White death held the universe in thrall. There was nothing at all save that still pale emptiness.

I was alone in an invisible universe, as if I floated through a white void.

Suddenly I thought, "What if Mary has called for me? What if she has sent a nurse to bring me to her, and I was not there?"

In something like a slow panic, I went back through the door to my bench, shuffling my feet so that I might be heard if anyone had been searching for me.

I sat down in the dim light, waiting, praying, staring at the mist pressing against the windows.

I waited for many hours; and for some part of that time, a kind of intermittent horror was added to my constant anxiety. Every now and then I heard a long rising and descending moan which echoed sepulchrally along the corridor.

Could that be Mary, I wondered? Could that be her voice, deepened by pain and by the high hollow tube of the corridor? It was a long time before I realized that I was merely hearing the loud and impolite yawning of some wakeful patient. And I could cheerfully have strangled him.

At last, at eternal last, the first intimations of dawn began to appear, changing the mist outside the windows from gray to white. I heard the purposeful tap-tapping of a woman's heels.

Peering along the corridor, I saw a white uniform advancing toward me like a welcome specter. I sat up tensely, waiting.

The uniform approached. It reached me. It passed. Not a word was spoken. The nurse did not seem to notice me.

I went limp.

Then the figure suddenly stopped and turned, as if struck with an afterthought. I heard a voice saying, "Oh, by the way—your wife just had a beautiful baby daughter. Everything's all right." And the nurse went on, receding from me, her heels tapping busily and efficiently.

I uttered the most idiotic question of my lifetime. *"Did she really?"* I called after the nurse, as if no such possibility ever had occurred to me; as if the idea of becoming a father were perfectly preposterous.

I have often wondered what that nurse thought. I have

wondered if she said to herself, as she walked away from me, that she must have delivered the message to the wrong man — perhaps to some husband who had brought his wife to the hospital for an emergency appendectomy, and was dumfounded by the extraordinary tidings about a childbirth.

I have wondered what the nurse thought; but there is no doubt about what I thought. I said to myself that no nurse could be so casual about bringing news so earth-shaking, if she realized that to a man who has sat through the night in a hospital corridor she comes as an annunciatory angel direct from the throne of God.

Well, of course, a nurse must be about her work. And of course, she grows accustomed to birth. People can grow accustomed to anything — even to the fact that out of the furnace of God's love, and a man's love, and a woman's love, there has come forth, glowing with the fires of creation, a new human being: a creature who will hold the stars in his eyes, and embrace a thousand universes with his mind, and live and die — and then go on living as long as God shall live, forever.

A nurse can grow accustomed even to such prodigies. She can grow so accustomed to them that she can say offhandedly, without raising her voice and without breaking her stride, that a child has been born. But I think that no man ever can get used to hearing that a child has been given to him and his wife.

Even while I was uttering my imbecilic exclamation, "Has she really?" the nurse was vanishing into another corridor, the tapping of her heels receding in the echoing distance. And there I sat, stunned by the thought that at last I was a father, and my wife a mother.

Presently the doctor came to me with a great smile and a firm congratulatory handclasp. He led me to Mary's room, and departed.

I cannot remember what Mary and I said to each other, or whether we said anything. Possibly I merely looked into her eyes, and she into mine, while we held hands in silence.

After a while, the hospital's obstetrician came in, beaming. In multisyllabled words, he said something about a nerve in the baby's head having been pinched with forceps, so that one eye wouldn't close. But it would close soon, he assured us cheerily.

Then, after some more technical talk, he went away, leaving us wondering what he had been trying to tell us.

We stopped wondering when a nurse came into the room with our daughter. We understood then why the obstetrician had tried to prepare us for a shock. The child was yellow with jaundice; one eye was closed in a pirate scowl; the other, wide open, glared accusingly at us. Black hair stuck up all over the oddly shaped little head.

Mary and I stared speechlessly at the apparition. Finally I said weakly to the nurse, "Are you sure this is the right baby?"

The nurse, smiling broadly, said she was sure, and went away with the little one. Mary and I stared at each other. The obstetrician, perhaps curious to know whether we had survived the shock, came in again, rubbing his hands, grinning happily, and asking how we liked the baby.

We informed him that "it" was one of the ugliest creatures we had ever laid eyes on. He drew himself up in injured dignity.

"I'll have you know," he said sternly, "that I deliver only

beautiful babies." Then he chuckled, and said, "The jaundice will go away. The eye will close. The head will grow nice and round. You'll see — she'll be a lovely baby."

We had our doubts. We were entirely prepared to love the ugliest baby on earth. We were happy to be the parents of the ugliest baby. We wouldn't have traded our ugly baby for all the beautiful babies on earth. We were prepared to take issue with anybody who dared agree with us that our ugly baby was not beautiful.

But as it turned out, she did grow to be a lovely baby. The obstetrician had been telling the truth. In a few weeks, our daughter was adorable, as he had promised. But it wouldn't have made any difference if he had been wrong. We hadn't been hoping and praying for a *beautiful* baby, but only for a real live baby.

7

EVERY DAY FOR TEN DAYS after the birth of our baby, I sent the *Vandergrift News* to press as early as possible, got into the Ford, and drove the twenty winding, hilly miles to the Allegheny Valley Hospital to visit my wife and child. I was allowed an hour with them in the afternoon, and another hour in the evening.

By cajoling the nurses, I was able often to stretch these periods into ninety minutes each. The month was June, and I spent the time between the afternoon and evening visits either sitting in a park, reading and watching the squirrels, or visiting fellow newspapermen on the *Allegheny Valley News* in Tarentum.

The publisher of the *Vandergrift News* — Herbert Brauff — was inexhaustibly patient with my absences. He understood; he had small children himself.

At the time this is written, it is customary to send a mother home from the hospital five days after a normal delivery, or even sooner. Not so in those earlier days: there was a kind of tradition that a woman must stay in bed at least nine days after a birth.

Our family doctor, Dr. Samuel Henderson, once told us of one woman whom he found in her yard hanging up the washing to dry, the day after her baby arrived. He decided that she had no need of his ministrations. More than a week later, however, he stopped to see her, just to be sure that everything was all right. She was in bed.

"Something wrong?" he asked her.

"No, no," she replied. "Everybody says, on the ninth day a woman must go to bed."

She was an immigrant who did not speak English well, and she had confused the nine-day tradition with "the ninth day."

Dr. Henderson was extremely happy over our baby. He had worked like a Trojan to save our first little one, and the child's death had been the first in his obstetrical experience. He had been as shocked as we were; and now he shared our joy.

He asked me, a few days after seeing me baptizing our first son, to teach him how to administer the Sacrament. He said, "If ever another Catholic child should die at birth while I am there, I'd like to do what the parents want done."

I explained that anybody could baptize, merely by intending to do what Christ wanted done, and saying, while pouring water on the person's skin, "I baptize thee in the Name of the Father, and of the Son, and of the Holy Ghost."

I remember that sometimes I had to defend Dr. Henderson when someone suggested that another doctor might have saved our first child. That was not true, and our best answer to the critics was our refusal to change physicians. We had utmost confidence in Dr. Henderson.

My mother-in-law rode to the hospital with me to bring home my wife and baby. She brought the clothing and blankets needed for the little one.

We rode through the green Pennsylvania hills in bright sunlight. My mother-in-law was serenely happy, I filled with a rollicking joy. We got Mary and the baby into the back seat, and on the way home I drove with meticulous care. Never were twenty miles traversed more carefully.

My brother, whose back was far stronger than mine, carried Mary up the twenty-five wooden steps to our flat, while I followed, holding the baby as if she were made of the most fragile glass. At last it was done. At last Mary sat smiling in a chair in the little parlor — the parlor where I had lolled on the floor, reading, in boyhood — and the baby was in a crib.

We were a family. The emptiness left by the death of our first-born was filled.

The Great Depression by this time was in full swing, and my father and mother had rented their house and moved into our flat, which in the meantime had been converted into two little apartments. Proudly, I escorted them into our apartment to see the baby.

My father sat down out of the eddy of excitement around the crib, looking on, smiling, from the edge of things. Suddenly I noticed him. I scooped up the infant and put Dad's first grandchild in his arms. Tears came into his eyes.

It was too soon for the other grandfather — Mary's father — to manifest more than a long-distance interest in the baby. Frank Hoffman was a great strong steelworker who could lift almost anything except an infant. He was terrified by these tiny creatures. After they grew old enough to walk, he never tired of being with them, but in the first year or two they were much too fragile to be held in his big hands.

He came to see our baby, but stood back from her, nodding his head on its great muscular neck and saying, "Nice. Nice. Too small for me. I'll wait until she's bigger."

That night, after Mary was asleep, I stood for a long time beside our baby's crib. Time after time I leaned close to her, listening to make sure that she was still breathing. Once I was so sure she wasn't that I poked her fearfully with a long index finger, and was rewarded by seeing her stir in her sleep.

How long I stood in the semidarkness, worrying about the little one's survival, I do not know. I remember that I felt a sudden special affinity with my patron, St. Joseph. I wondered whether he had stayed awake half the night in the stable at Bethlehem, listening for the Christ Child's breathing.

Presently I decided that I could leave our little one in God's care. I undressed silently, slid into bed, and closed my eyes in sleep.

Next day was the Fourth of July, Independence Day — a holiday. Some time in the early morning I was awakened by the baby's fussing. I rose and fed her, lulled her to sleep, and crawled back into bed. Not long afterward, I was aroused by my mother shaking my shoulder. She spoke in the tone of one announcing a crisis. "Get up, Joseph, get up! There are a lot of diapers to be washed."

Why she did that to me, and why I allowed it to be done to me, I have never understood; nor has Mary. We can only guess that my mother must have been overexcited about being a grandmother. There were plenty of clean garments for the baby; there was no reason for waking me from a sound sleep and putting me to scrubbing diapers on a washboard in the bathroom — on Independence Day! — instead of doing them later in the electric washer.

I scrubbed until my knuckles were raw, and not until much later did I realize how I had been put upon.

The next Sunday, I went with the sponsors to church and watched while our baby was baptized. We named her Mary after her mother and the Mother of Mothers. I thought again of the ancient blessing that had been called down upon us by Father Edgar: "Thy children shall be as olive-plants around about thy table."

Now we had the first of our olive plants, and in baptism she had been made a child of God, a coheir with Christ to the kingdom of heaven. God was beginning to fulfill His blessings in us. We were starting to increase and multiply according to His commandment.

My wife, for no particular reason, had an affectionate way of calling small babies "Betsy." She did so with our little one who, as she began to talk, rendered the name "Bussie." This was a convenience, avoiding the confusion that can arise when mother and daughter have the same name. In our case the confusion would have been twice confounded, because Mary was also the name of my wife's mother and of one of my sisters — the one in the convent.

Bussie proved to be inventive in surmounting such difficulties. She called her mother "Mommie," herself "Bussie," and my mother "Grandma." The other grandmother became "Munner." My father was "Grandpa," and Mary's father "Poppie." My sister was dubbed "Sister Auntie Mary." These appellations were adopted all around, so that everybody knew who was meant when a name was mentioned.

Bussie suffered the disadvantage of being the first baby — the baby everybody bothers, and the one upon whom the parents practice at being parents. We invested endless hours in feeding, bathing, sterilizing, and clothing her. She was much fussed with, and she had colic for months. Mary and I walked the floor with her until we were blind for sleep.

We were a bewildered father and mother, unable to understand what was wrong with our child — although Dr. Henderson did tell us one day, with a grin, that the only thing wrong with the baby was her possession of four grandparents and a lot of other relatives.

We will never forget one night — or rather early morning — when Mary and I, utterly exhausted, fell asleep lying crosswise across a bed, with Bussie between us. We awoke that way in the late morning, all three much refreshed by the first good sleep we had had in weeks.

Often we placed our howling Bussie on a pillow, carried her down the long flight of steps, got into the Ford, and drove hither and yon through the night. Bussie slept as long as the car was moving and thus we won some respite from her crying. But sometimes we were near to desperation when she would wake, howling, merely because we had paused for a stop light.

Perhaps our most puzzled moment came when Bussie was about nine months old. By that time, she was occupying her high chair at meals with us, eating crushed vegetables, apple sauce, and the like, and grunting and pointing at things on the table which she wished to sample. One day she grunted and pointed while I was drinking milk. I poured some in a glass and gave her a drink.

That night, when we offered Bussie her bedtime bottle, she struck it away angrily, howling her protests. We tried everything to soothe her, but each time she was offered the bottle she staged the same wrathy rebellion. We decided that something must be wrong with the formula. Wearily, we went to the kitchen and made a new batch. We offered it to Bussie, and she struck it away with a new outburst of crying.

We were at our wits' end. We stood staring in bewilderment at each other above the crib with its howling infant. Suddenly I remembered the glass of milk. "I'll bet the little rascal wants it out of a glass," I said. "She wants to drink the grown-up way."

I got a tumbler, poured the milk formula into it, sat Bussie upright, and offered the glass to her. She seized my hand and drank greedily, as gratified as a politician who has just heard his opponent concede defeat.

All through her childhood, Bussie demonstrated this independent desire to have done with the things of infancy as early as possible. By the time she was eight or nine years old, she was able to do all the shopping for groceries and meat without help. This proved to be a happy circumstance during a long period when her mother was too ill to discharge more than the absolute minimum of household duties.

8

THE DEPRESSION forced me suddenly and unexpectedly to assume entire responsibility for the *Vandergrift News*, where before I had been merely a writing reporter and a kind of apprentice editor. The newspaper's income declined disastrously as the steel industry went into the doldrums.

The big steel plant along the river, which had thundered through the days and nights of my boyhood and young manhood, fell nearly silent. The fortnightly payrolls which were the town's chief means of support declined disastrously, until Vandergrift was "making do" with one tenth of its normal income.

In my high school days, I had worked for some months in the steel plant as a laborer on the open hearth. So great was the demand for steel at that time that junior and senior high school lads were invited to work five hours each night after school, and thirteen hours on Friday nights — Saturday being our free day. I was among those who responded.

It was a valuable experience. In hours when our work had been done, we were permitted to wander through the plant, seeing the entire operation, and asking questions of the men at the great machines.

I came to understand how steel was made, from the first

operation of melting ore and mixing it with the proper ingredients in the inferno of the open-hearth furnaces, through the pouring, the rolling of ingots, and the rolling and cutting of bars and sheets.

Strangely enough, I enjoyed laboring in the steel plant, although the work was hard, sweaty, and incredibly dirty. With deafeningly chattering air hammers, we tore down the "checkers" under the furnaces when they were clogged with slag. We delivered material for new furnaces, tossing brick from a railroad car, catching them in our leather-protected hands, and stacking them. We became proud of our skill in sailing them two at a time so that they did not separate and pinch the hands of the receiver as he plucked them out of the air. We loaded and unloaded ore, manganese and dolomite — the latter a powdery substance that raised an acrid, choking dust and sometimes made our noses bleed.

A high and dramatic moment was the tapping of a furnace. We would gather when the word went around, and watch the "second helper" as he probed cunningly at the plug which held at bay tons of bubbling, flaming metal. Suddenly the plug would give way, the man would leap aside, and a torrent of blinding-hot steel would gush from the furnace into a huge ladle.

Most of us had had, at one time or another, the experience of being ordered by some humorous subforeman to go down on the "floor" and bring him a ladle. This was a standard joke — the ladles being thirty or forty feet in height, and movable only by the enormous electric cranes that ran on tracks far above us, under the roof of the plant.

My understanding, thus gained, of the kind of work which engaged most of the male population of Vandergrift

was helpful to me in handling many stories in our newspaper, and in selecting the kind of news which would be
of most value to our readers.

As a reporter-editor, I was often away from home late at
night. Mary, however, never complained. The monthly ses-
sions of the Town Council, which I attended, normally
went on into the small hours of the morning. Often they
were deadly dull, but occasionally they produced something
to be treasured.

I remember one councilman pounding the table and de-
manding that a favor be granted to a concern which had
rendered a number of services to our town. In measured
tones, he insisted:

"Gentlemen, I tell you these people have corporated with
us, and it's only fair for us to retaliate."

Perhaps the most wonderful use of the English language
I have ever heard, however, came from the chairman of a
committee appointed by the Town Council to wait upon me
in the offices of the *Vandergrift News* and lodge an official
complaint against one of our headlines.

The headline said that the council, at its meeting the
night previous, had ignored some problem or other that was
troubling the citizens.

I was astonished at being approached by an official committee on the subject of a headline. But my astonishment
changed to utter bafflement as we talked for fifteen or
twenty minutes at cross purposes. I failed completely in my
efforts to learn what the committee was objecting to. The
chairman kept insisting that the headline was false, and
I insisted that it was true.

Finally the chairman slapped the front page with his

hand and said loudly, "I tell you that headline is a lie! It says we ignored this matter. We did not ignore it. We simply did not discuss it at all."

At last we understood each other, and I was able to soothe the committeemen and send them away reasonably happy by explaining that I had used the word "ignore" to mean that they "simply hadn't discussed the matter at all." Just a mix-up in terminology, I indicated, restraining myself from smiling.

Every newspaperman learns soon enough that there are ten thousand traps concealed in word usages. I have often told budding young journalists that the most valuable knowledge an experienced newsman possesses cannot be taught to others because it consists largely in a sixth sense which keeps him from saying the wrong thing, or the ambiguous thing, or the unintentionally insulting thing. "The best things you learn in this business," I tell cub reporters, "are things you can't teach to anybody else because you really don't know that you know them yourself. Knowing what not to do is far more important than knowing what to do."

I liked to get news firsthand, and often in those days Tackle McIntyre or some other policeman telephoned me in the witching hours to tell me to hurry to the scene of a murder, a robbery, or an accident. Frequently, too, I rode the fire trucks to fires and busily gathered information while the streams of water were turned on the flames. I was not able to adopt the philosophy of an earlier publisher for whom I had worked when the *Vandergrift News* was a weekly.

He was a man of gigantic girth and weight, barely able to fit enough of himself into an office chair to support him at his desk. One day he inquired of me, "Joe, I hear that you jump out of bed at night and ride with the firemen to fires."

I admitted it.

"Poof," he said, his great belly shaking with laughter. "Do you know what I do when the fire siren sounds?"

"No."

"I roll over in bed and feel the wall with my hand. If the wall isn't hot, I go back to sleep. What do you think the telephone's for? You can always get your information the next day."

I did not heed his advice. After all, he was a prodigiously portly man in late middle age. I was a lean greyhound of a chap in my twenties. It made a difference.

Mary endured endless shoptalk in the evenings, when one or more of the other men on the paper came to our little apartment to visit. She sat smiling and listening, and seldom did she suggest that there might possibly be some other topic of conversation beside newspapering.

She did, however, object mildly when I began playing chess frequently with Joe Robinson, a young professor in the local high school. I could not blame her; we sat sometimes for half an hour or more without uttering a sound, absorbed in our study of the chessmen's positions. Fortunately, we gradually lost interest in the game. We were too active physically to enjoy sitting still for so long.

When the Depression reached its deepest depths, our publisher, Herbert Brauff, called me into his office one day and announced that he was taking an executive position on another newspaper in a distant city in order to relieve the *News* of the weight of his salary. "I'll leave you in charge," he said.

I found myself suddenly entirely responsible for both the editorial and the business sides of a daily newspaper. Never before had I given more than a passing thought to anything except the gathering and writing of news.

Soon enough I discovered that the situation was just as bad as it could be. We were pell-melling into complete bankruptcy. Our expenses were far exceeding our earnings every week. Unless something drastic was done, we faced disaster.

I called a meeting of everybody connected with the paper. We gathered in the publisher's office, draping ourselves on the desk, the radiators, the window sills. As briefly as possible I gave the staff the appalling facts about our financial situation.

"From now on," I told them, "it's simply a matter of survival. We're all in the same boat. We've got to forget about titles and positions. Either we all cut our pay to a bare subsistence level, or we end up jobless, with no income at all. I say we ought to divide up the available income according to each one's need, and ride out this storm. It's better than finding ourselves walking the streets without any salaries at all."

They agreed. I cut my own salary from $45 weekly to $14, and adjusted the others similarly. Even so, there were to be times before the Depression began to lift, when even the pittances we had assigned ourselves could be paid only partially.

The greatest crisis came when a company from which we had bought paper for years suddenly demanded full payment of the back account before any more paper would be delivered. I left the editing of the paper to a couple of young assistants, Byron Campbell and Kenneth Speer, and spent my days for more than a week going from merchant to merchant, begging for payments on their advertising bills.

"Either I get in enough money to pay the paper bill," I told them, "or the *News* closes its doors, and this town is left without a newspaper — and you without an advertising medium."

They responded nobly, and at last I had enough funds to cover the paper account. The paper company dispatched a carload of newsprint, and then the question faced us: "Will the paper arrive before our stock is exhausted?"

It did — but at the last dramatic moment. I came to the office one morning and was told by the pressman, Marty Sinnott, that we had enough paper to print only a few hundred copies. "Unless that carload arrives today," he said, "we're sunk."

Three o'clock came — press time — and still no paper. We were telephoning the railroad station every fifteen minutes. We started the press and ran off the last roll of paper. Marty stopped the press and stood looking at me helplessly.

Suddenly I remembered that during the Christmas season, we had printed hundreds of thousands of handbills in many colors. I asked Marty, "Don't we have some tag ends and bobtails of colored rolls left?"

He stared at me as if I had lost my mind. "But the colors!" he protested.

"Devil with the colors. People will think we're starting something new."

We found enough rolls to finish that day's run — even though the *Vandergrift News* did come out in pink, green, yellow, and blue.

But that was that. We hadn't a scrap of paper left.

Next day, we telephoned again and again to the railroad station. Always we got the discouraging answer, "Not here yet."

We went ahead with the writing of news and headlines. We set the type as usual, placed it in the forms, locked it up, and set the forms in place on the flat-bed press.

Three o'clock. Press time. And there we were, all standing around the press, staring at the clock — and no paper.

We had a truck waiting at the freight depot. At a few minutes after 3, the telephone rang. "The paper's here," said the truck driver.

"Load one roll and rush it here as fast as you can," I told him. "You can deliver the rest of it afterward."

We stood around cheering and slapping one another on the back as the paper was rolled into the building, jockeyed into place, and threaded through the press. Marty started the motor and pulled his lever, and papers began to come off the press. The *Vandergrift News* had not missed an edition. Hurrah!

But Mary to this day occasionally tells of waking one night to find me sitting up in bed in my sleep, shouting at some imaginary creditor, "But I tell you, you can't have the money! There just *isn't* any money!"

During this Depression period, my father had gone bankrupt, closed his store and electrical business, and lost his building to a thoroughly heartless mortgage company which declined to accept interest without payments on principal during the emergency.

Even now, I find it difficult to forgive that building and loan outfit, and although I like almost everybody I have ever met, I entertain a profound distaste for the loan manager who brushed father and me off coldly and unfeelingly when we suggested that he accept interest only until Dad could get his business on its feet. I will never forget the lofty manner in which that man repeated, as we explained our plight to him, "That's not my problem." I can understand why some revolutionists become revolutionists.

After Dad's building was taken by the building and loan

company, Mary and I and Bussie moved to a little house a mile or so outside Vandergrift, in a lane off a highway at the bottom of a steep hill. There, for a while, one of Mary's sisters and her three children lived with us while her husband looked for a job.

The Works Progress Administration, through which the government at last moved to help the unemployed, came to Vandergrift on a bitter winter's day. The temperature was forty or fifty degrees below freezing.

I looked up from my typewriter and saw a group of men shoveling snow from the sidewalks outside our building. I went outside and asked what they were doing. "Working for the WPA," they said. Among them were two or three professional men.

Some were not dressed for weather so cold. While I was interviewing them and taking notes, I glanced furtively at the foreman and told the men in a low voice, "Take turns dodging into our building to warm up. If you don't, you'll all come down with pneumonia."

Through the long day, they came in and out, blue with cold, stamping their feet and rubbing their half-frozen hands. They were too weary and cold to be especially cheerful, but they were happy to be earning something for their families.

In our little house in the little suburb oddly called Oklahoma, Mary and I and Bussie, and Mary's sister and her three children managed magically with my $14 weekly income. Each payday, I negotiated with a vegetable man who gave me great quantities of vegetables for a few dollars. At meat and grocery stores, I tried to exchange advertising in the paper for foodstuffs. When I failed, I handed over, reluctantly, the necessary cash.

Piling everything into the back seat of the Ford, I chugged up the steep hill through Vandergrift Heights and down the other side into Oklahoma.

Each Saturday evening, I was greeted enthusiastically as I carried food into the house and deposited it in the kitchen. The four children clustered around to see what I had brought in the way of cookies or doughnuts or candy. My wife and her sister delved curiously into packages and boxes.

Despite our Depression-born difficulties, we were happy. And we were never really hungry. Mary's sister had a genius for baking and cooking in such fashion as to stretch the food as far as possible. We learned from her what magnificent soups can be made at small expense from bones, small cuts of meat, and vegetables.

In this little house in Oklahoma, Mary's time came again. We rode in the Ford once more to Allegheny Valley Hospital. I had not waited long when the hospital's obstetrician came to me, looking grave.

We had lost another child. But this time there was little shock. We had prepared our minds for disappointment; we had schooled ourselves to wait upon the event, and to expect nothing. I rode up in the elevator with the obstetrician and walked into the delivery room. I remember well the sympathetic eyes of several nurses.

For a moment, I stood gazing down at the body of our little one, a girl whom we later named Bernadine after my sister who had died in childhood. Then I looked up as Dr. Henderson spoke. "I didn't wait for you, Joe. There wasn't time. I baptized the baby immediately, just as you taught me."

It was the first infant he had ever baptized.

9

A GREAT CHANGE IN OUR LIVES began after the Depression eased, and Herbert Brauff resumed his position as publisher of the paper. One day he called me into his office and said grimly — his grimness being caused, I am sure, by his distaste for what he was doing — "Joe, you don't belong on the *Vandergrift News*. I think I ought to kick you upstairs."

I did not know exactly what he meant, although I understood the expression. He went on, "You are a good writer, and you like to write. But that's all you like to do. You're interested only in the big stories. The backbone of a small-town paper is the small news — the little items about people. That sort of thing bores you."

He was making a magnificent understatement. I found it intolerable to gather what we called "personals," and to listen to the dozens of women who telephoned each day to tell us that "Mrs. Smith went shopping in Pittsburgh," or "Mrs. Jones visited her daughter in Sugar Creek," or "Miss Brown is planning a double-ring ceremony for her wedding."

There was one woman who telephoned me religiously each evening just as Mary and I were having dinner. Her husband was an important person in Vandergrift, and she had to be catered to. But she talked incessantly and endlessly, in a constant stream broken only by an occasional aside to her husband: "Isn't that so, Precious?"

I have long been puzzled by the diabolical influence which telephones exercise on many women. A housewife, with whom one can carry on a normal give-and-take conversation face to face, will suddenly be stricken with a kind of pox of words the moment she lifts a telephone receiver. But this woman was the most inveterate talker in all my experience. She spoke rapidly, shrilly, pointlessly, and tirelessly. She was bedeviled with words. I pitied her husband greatly.

For a while, I listened patiently each evening, letting my dinner grow cold, and signaling to Mary to bring a chair to the telephone so that I could seat myself during the terrible ordeal. Then Mary began to spell me. After I had endured the torture for fifteen or twenty minutes, she would take my place and hold the receiver to her ear while I ate.

Finally, we realized that the woman did not really know whether anybody was listening or not, and that she did not hear our occasional brief "uh-huhs" or "yeses." She needed no encouragement, she needed no answers. She needed only the telephone mouthpiece before her. It was as if she suffered from some dread affliction that could be alleviated only by pouring thousands of words into that uncomplaining instrument. We discovered that we could let the telephone receiver dangle and go on peacefully eating while the torrent of words flowed on.

Finally the woman would stop and cut the connection, unaware that she had been talking to nobody.

Such annoyances are routine in the life of small-town newspapermen, and I salute them for their preternatural patience. But I had no such patience; I wanted to write. I was filled with thoughts that I wanted to get on paper. Yet

I understood what Herbert Brauff was saying; I knew that small newspapers cannot compete with metropolitan papers on big news, and must hold their circulation by publishing the little things that are so important to individuals.

"I am going to kick you upstairs," Herbert Brauff repeated. "I had lunch with the managing editor of the *Pittsburgh Sun-Telegraph* the other day. He was saying that he had searched high and low for a good writer, and hadn't found one. I told him I had a man who could write as well as the best man on his staff. He said, 'Then for heaven's sake send him to me!'"

I was now doubly startled. It was a shock to me to be told that I could compete on even terms with big-city newsmen. I had thought of them as lordly beings, far above me in ability. After all, I was a small-town boy, and had never thought about being anything else. Big cities frightened me, and I was deeply disturbed at the thought of living and working in one.

I concealed my agitation, however. I nodded sagely, as if in complete agreement with my boss. "Would you like to work on the *Sun-Telegraph?*" he asked.

I said yes, but my heart wasn't in it. Nevertheless, the die was cast. I went home that evening and told Mary, and I could almost see her heart sinking. But she took the blow courageously, as she has taken every disappointment from the beginning of our married life.

For two or three months, I commuted between Vandergrift and Pittsburgh, taking a very early morning train, and arriving home in the evening barely in time for an hour or two with Mary before bedtime. I had always been thin, but now I became gaunt.

Each week end, despite foul winter weather, we drove to Pittsburgh in the Ford to hunt an apartment. It was a discouraging business. Some of the places we were offered for what we could afford to pay were unfit for human habitation.

At last my Sister-sister came to our rescue. This was my sister Mary, who has been a kind of counselor and goad to me since my boyhood. She has always been very unlike me — competent where I was bungling, confident where I was diffident, gregarious where I was retiring, at home with people where I was embarrassed with them, and swift to make decisions and take action where I was hesitant and dreamy.

My sister Mary had encouraged me to write even in boyhood. She had insisted that I could become an author, although to me that seemed like trying to become an angel. To me, being an author was the greatest height to which a human being could aspire. I wanted to be an author more than I wanted to be anything else on earth; but I thought it impossible. My sister said, "Bosh. Of course you can be a writer. You've got talent; all you've got to do is develop it."

She cast the die for me when I entered high school as a freshman. She was then secretary to the superintendent of schools. I had written some short stories, and she suggested that I submit them to the editor of the high school magazine, *The Spectator*.

The idea appalled me. "I'm only a freshman," I protested. "I can't compete with seniors and juniors. The editor would think my stories were childish."

I flatly refused to submit them. I could imagine the editor laughing; and I couldn't endure the thought of my stories being laughed at.

The editor's name, it seems to me, was Kenneth Thompson. My sister secretly filched a couple of my stories from me, and handed them to him. He accepted them for publication.

I was overwhelmed when my sister told me. It was unthinkable that I was to see my stories in print. But I did see them — and from that moment I was lost. I had to be a writer.

I began "thinking stories" day and night. I took long walks, inventing tales and turning sentences over and over in my mind. I lay awake at night, doing the same thing.

In class, I could hardly pay attention to the teachers. My mind went wandering off into the fields of literary creation. In study hall, I put aside my books and wrote stories. I determined that I would have a story or an article in every issue of *The Spectator* from the beginning of my freshman year to the day of graduation. I believe I accomplished that.

All this time, strangely enough, I was taking a science course with the vague intention of becoming an electrical engineer. This idea had been put into my head by my mother. Originally she had wanted me to be a priest, but my two years at St. Vincent's had demonstrated that I had no religious vocation.

I recall that when I was five or six years old, I had told my mother that I guessed I would be a priest. Not long afterward, our pastor, Father Linus, visited our home.

I remember him sitting, a giant of a man, in a rocking chair in our little parlor. My mother, unwisely enthusiastic over what she imagined was my vocation, called me in from the dining room and said proudly, "Joseph, tell Father Linus what you are going to be when you grow up."

What perversity seized me at that moment, I cannot guess. But I stood before Father Linus and said, "I'm going to drive a garbage cart."

Never have I heard a man laugh as Father Linus did. He exploded; he strangled with laughter. His face got red, and tears ran down his cheeks. Finally he patted my head and told me that he hoped I'd make a good garbage driver. Then he exploded again, and I sidled out of the room, wondering what in the world had struck him as being so funny.

Giving up hope of seeing me at the altar, mother next suggested electrical engineering.

I signed for the science course in high school, and went through with it. There was a strange separation in my mind all this time. I wanted to be an author, but I took it for granted that I would be an electrical engineer first.

The evening before Commencement Day, I was strolling along a Vandergrift street with the president of the senior class, a highly competent and intelligent Jewish youth named Harold Schuler. He asked whether I intended to go to college.

I said yes, I was going to the University of Notre Dame. This was more of my sister Mary's doing. She had determined that I ought to go to Notre Dame, and had convinced me by taking me to Forbes Field in Pittsburgh to see the blue-and-gold clad Fighting Irish defeat Carnegie Tech on the gridiron.

To me at that age, a college was judged by its football team. If Notre Dame had a better team than Carnegie Tech, then to Notre Dame I would go. My first year there, by the way, was the beginning of the reign of the Four Horsemen — Crowley, Miller, Stuhldreher, and Layden.

My Jewish friend inquired what course I was going to take in college. "Electrical engineering," I replied matter-of-factly.

He stopped walking and stared at me. "What!"

"What's wrong with that?" I asked. "My mother says electrical engineers make good salaries."

"But Joe!" he protested. "Look at your high school record!"

"What about it?"

"Why, man — you're no good in algebra, no good in arithmetic, no good in science, not much good in geometry —. Engineering isn't your field."

I spread my hands helplessly. "What, then?"

He put his hand on my arm. "You're the best writer this high school has ever had. Everybody says that."

"They do?"

"Certainly. Writing is what you're interested in, isn't it?"

"Yes. But I can't make a living writing."

"You can make a living while you're learning to write."

"How?"

"Joe, I think you're a born newspaperman."

It was as if he had turned on a light in my head. "Of course!" I exclaimed. "That's what I ought to be!"

I went home and told my mother. She looked at me as if I had said I was going to be a burglar. But she allowed me to write to Notre Dame and request admittance to the School of Journalism.

The Dean of the school — and at that time almost the entire faculty — was John Cooney. He was one of the gentlest men I have ever known. His courses consisted largely in handing out assignments for us to cover, and in devoting the class period to philosophizing about life. Oddly enough, he produced some eminently successful journalists.

I can see him rubbing his bald spot and smiling his benign smile while he peered at us through his spectacles, which were always sliding to the end of his nose, far below his bushy eyebrows.

"Boys," he would say, "always be gentlemen. Always be Notre Dame gentlemen. If you drink, drink like gentlemen. If you have visitors, receive them like a gentleman. Don't open the door a crack and peer out at them as if they were gangsters. Swing the door wide and welcome them. Be gentlemen when you cover your stories. Be gentlemen when you interview somebody. Be gentlemen always to women. Gentlemen — gentlemen — always be gentlemen!"

We loved Doc Cooney.

All through my college years, as through my high school time, my sister goaded me to write. She made me promise, when I left for Notre Dame, that I would begin submitting stories to the college magazine immediately. I did so, and they were accepted in *The Scholastic*, as they had been in *The Spectator*.

I could not understand why. My stuff seemed to me pretty poor. I was flabbergasted when I was invited to join The Scribblers, an exclusive group of campus writers sponsored by the legendary Charles Phillips, who taught literature and was himself a poet.

I was equally flabbergasted, in my junior year, to be made editor of *The Scholastic* on the insistence of the graduating editor, Bill Dooley. I could hardly believe that Bill had recommended me, and no one else.

Thus did my sister push and prod me into successes of which I had never dreamed. In the meantime, she had become, first, secretary to a surgeon in Pittsburgh and then a Sister of Charity — Sister Regina Clare — at Seton Hill, in Greensburg, our county seat.

And now, when Mary and I were searching for an apartment, Sister Regina was teaching at Sacred Heart parish school in Pittsburgh. One day she telephoned to say that she had found an apartment for us across the street from the church. Our search was ended.

We moved in, and entered into an entirely new life.

10

THE BEAUTY OF RELIGION now became visible to us for the first time. For the first time, too, we began to discover its magnificent intellectual content. Religion was not a mere matter of "do not do this, do not do that."

The faith, we learned, had the true and elevating answers to all human perplexities. Its genius really lay not in the realm of the negative, but in the realm of the positive. What it actually was saying to people, and saying it over and over, was "Come up higher, friend. Rise to real happiness and to the enduring joys."

Mary and I had grown up in a parish that was as polyglot as possible. The pastor was busy with the everyday labor of ministering to his people. If he got them to Mass on Sundays, if he heard their confessions, baptized their babies, administered the sacraments to the dying, and buried the dead, he was doing all that could be expected of one man. There was no time for books, for inquiry and discussion classes and clubs, for the great music and art of the Church.

Each Sunday, the poor man had to preach several sermons in several tongues at several Masses. And he was not a linguist. He spoke first in English, and then stumbled through exhortations and instructions in Polish and Italian, and sometimes in a fourth language.

At least once a month, furthermore, he had to read the list of contributors to the collection, and the amount given by each.

It was pitiful and intolerably tiring to hear him trying to pronounce names filled with s's and z's, pausing while he studied each name, and finally having a go at saying it — after which, as likely as not, he had to utter the awful anti-climax: "ten cents," or "twenty-five cents."

He went through this ordeal earnestly, trying to say each name clearly. He knew, as did we, that often the dime or the quarter, carefully placed in an envelope and dropped into the basket, represented a real sacrifice. He was always careful to thank the people for their generosity after plowing through the endless list.

But what with the three or four sermons, and the reading of contributions and announcements of deaths, marriages, parish card parties, and the like, the Sunday Masses were long, tiring affairs. As often as not, we sat through them trying not to take a deep breath, because many of our fellow parishioners were addicted to garlic. Apparently they breakfasted before Mass, and sometimes it seemed to me that the breakfasts must have consisted mostly of garlic. The atmosphere was overpowering.

Now, after moving to Pittsburgh, we found ourselves attending what I shall take the liberty of considering, until someone proves otherwise, the most beautiful church in the world. Sacred Heart was Father Thomas F. Coakley's labor of love; and Father Coakley was the most uncompromising perfectionist I have ever met.

Before the church was designed, he and his architect, his builder, and his stained-glass man traveled the length of

Europe from Scotland into the boot of Italy, examining every famous basilica, cathedral, shrine, and parish church, and many that seldom are heard of. Plans and drawings were dug out of half-forgotten files and examined.

Father Coakley was determined that his church would embody the best to be found in any other church anywhere, and yet would be an edifice of perfect unity. I am convinced that he achieved his ambition.

Sacred Heart, to me, combines an unearthly and an earthly beauty. In mass and proportion it is like a mountain, and yet it soars in splendid arches. Its majesty is almost the majesty of divine presence. Its jeweled glass windows fill it with a colored mist.

I was so entranced with the church that I took to spending hours there, studying the curve of this arch, the vista along that aisle, the grace of one statue or another. Sometimes I sat simply soaking in the beauty of the sanctuary. Or I stood admiring the play of light and shadow on the great rose window as clouds passed across the sun outside.

We came to know Father Coakley well. We listened avidly as he told the history of the church, showed plans and designs that had been considered and discarded — and told why — and displayed little model stained-glass windows which had been studied for weeks in various qualities of daylight before one color or another had been approved for the Sacred Heart windows.

But Father Coakley's conversation was not confined to the subject of his church. He had a scintillating mind and a whiplike wit, and his interests ranged through science and philosophy and theology and economics and politics.

The old house in which he and his assistants lived bulged

with books, and often, in midsentence, he would leap from his chair, snatch a volume from a shelf, open it, and hand us a passage to read. Usually he dusted the book first with the skirt of his cassock, remarking humorously on the wisdom of the Church in dressing priests in black for such emergencies.

One of Father Coakley's assistants was the extraordinary Father Victor Kennedy, a dumpling of a man with a quietly indomitable fund of courage, and a childlike wisdom. He had not the slightest trace of Father Coakley's brilliance, and sometimes Father Coakley would remark, with a smile, "That man drives me mad." Immediately, however, he would add, "But he's the greatest priest in the country." Then he would tell a story about Father Kennedy.

Sometimes the story concerned Father Kennedy's mysterious success in bringing a convert into the faith after Father Coakley and the other priests had dismally failed. Nobody was able to understand this. Father Kennedy's instructions in Catholic teaching were halting, hawing, and humming affairs. Half the time it almost seemed as if he himself needed instruction. But the converts loved him, and came into the Church in a steady stream. They themselves were at a loss to explain why.

Once Father Coakley told of having received a telephone call from a woman who said she was locked in a room. Her husband, in a drunken rage, was outside, trying to break in, vowing to bind her and kill her with a butcher knife. Father Coakley was unable to leave at the moment, and relayed the message to Father Kennedy. The rolypoly little man nodded, went outside, and got into his automobile. An hour later, he returned, laid a butcher knife and a coil of rope on Father

Coakley's desk, and went upstairs to his room without a word. He refused ever to discuss the matter."

I went with Father Kennedy in his car one day while he made some visitations around the parish. Priests are notoriously individualistic drivers, but never have I taken a ride as peculiar as that one. Father Kennedy was oblivious of stop signs and traffic lights. Halfway through a right turn, he was as likely as not to change his mind suddenly and decide to go left. He invariably started the car with a jerk, and stopped it as if it had crashed into a stone wall.

At last we got back to Sacred Heart rectory. Inside, I parted from Father Kennedy. I went up the stairs to the room of another assistant pastor, Father Howard Carroll. I knocked, entered, sank into a chair, and said, "Whew!"

Father Carroll looked up from a book. "What's up?"

"I've just escaped from Father Kennedy's car."

He stared. "Don't tell me you went riding with *that* man?"

I nodded.

"Didn't you know what kind of driver he is?"

"If I had, do you think I would have gone with him?"

Father Carroll shook his head wonderingly. "I thought everybody in the city had heard about Father Kennedy's driving. Why, he's got seven special guardian angels to keep him from harm. That's because of his innocence; he really doesn't know that he can't drive an auto. But God expects other people to have enough sense not to ride with him."

"God can depend on me from now on," I assured him.

Father Carroll was chiefly responsible for the great change that took place in our religious life after we moved to Pittsburgh. He and Mary and I became close friends. We spent hours in discussion. I accompanied him often on his evening visits to his mother's home, where usually we were joined by his brother, Father Coleman Carroll.

The third brother, also a priest, I never met. Until his death some fifteen years later, Father Walter Carroll was stationed in Rome, with the Vatican secretariate of state.

From the first moment I met Mrs. Carroll, I knew that I was in the presence of a remarkable person. I was not surprised that she had given three priests to the Church. In her there was not the faintest trace of the tentativeness, the indecisiveness, the irresolution which handicap most of us. She struck me as being like the Church — built on a rock.

Her common sense was gigantic; her faith deep, practical, and indomitable. When I was in her home, seated at her kitchen table drinking coffee and eating cookies with Father Howard and Father Coleman, I was careful to try to avoid saying anything foolish or trivial. That sort of thing seemed entirely out of place.

Not that Mrs. Carroll lacked humor; she didn't. But she faced bravely and constantly the full reality of existence — a reality that included the omnipresence of God, and the awe-inspiring fact that one's business in life was to prepare for eternal life with Him. I never heard her utter a single piety; but in her presence I felt as if huge virtues were standing around me and looking silently down upon me.

From childhood I had been an omnivorous reader, but my chief source of material had been the public library in my home town. Now I began to discover the immense treasures of Catholic literature.

Father Carroll's room was more than lined with books. It was nearly buried in books. They were stacked everywhere —

on his desk, on a table, on chairs, on the floor. I began to borrow those which he recommended, and to devour them at home.

Night after night I lay awake reading, often until the wee hours of the morning, while Mary and Bussie slumbered. Years afterward, I elicited appreciative chuckles from a priest-editor of a magazine by remarking to him that at a certain period of my life I had realized that I was nearly a pagan in my thinking, and that I had therefore decided "to Catholicize my mind."

"That's *good!*" he said. "'Catholicize your mind.' Quite an expression. I'll have to remember that."

In the city room of the *Sun-Telegraph* one day, one of the assistant city editors, Fuzzy (Bill) Pfarr, said to me in his short, brusque way, "Write us an Ash Wednesday story."

I began the story with the injunction uttered by the priest when he makes the Sign of the Cross on one's forehead with ashes: "Remember, man, that thou art dust, and unto dust thou shalt return."

Fuzzy read the story and asked abruptly, "Where'd you get this quotation?"

"That's what the priests say on Ash Wednesday," I told him.

"Where'd you get it?" he repeated.

"Out of my head."

He glared at me. "Out of your head? You mean you didn't check it with anybody?"

"No need to check it," I assured him. "It's correct."

He tossed the story in front of me. "Just the same, check it."

I got Father Coakley on the telephone. Fuzzy Pfarr picked

up a connecting phone and listened. I asked Father Coakley for a translation of the Latin phrase spoken by priests while they are administering the ashes on Ash Wednesday.

Father Coakley gave it to me as I had written it. I thanked him, and hung up the receiver.

Fuzzy looked at me curiously. "How come you knew that quotation by heart?"

"Heavens, Fuzzy, I don't forget things like that."

"Even when you *know* something," he warned me, "check it."

Nevertheless, he seemed somewhat impressed by my accurate knowledge of the quotation.

After a few similar incidents, always involving fairly elementary facts about "things Catholic," I found myself accepted, by unspoken consent, as a kind of "Catholic expert" in the city room.

Not every question that arose, however, was elementary. One evening I was sprawling in a chair in Father Carroll's room, listening to his account of the many hours he devoted to instructing converts. Suddenly I said, "Maybe you ought to think about instructing some of the born Catholics, too."

"Why do you say that?"

I spread my hands. "Look at me. The fellows at the *Sun-Tele* are always coming around with questions — and half of them I can't answer adequately."

"Let's start a study club," said Father Carroll.

"What's that?"

"You get five or six people together, and I'll show you."

That was the beginning of what came to be known as "The Sheep and Goats," a lively weekly discussion group which grew rapidly, split into two groups, and to this day has not ceased generating new groups for study of Christian doctrine and Christian solutions to modern problems.

The first gathering consisted of myself and one or two other Catholics, a couple of Protestants, and an unbeliever. I persuaded the non-Catholics to attend by assuring them that we needed "Devil's Advocates."

"What's a Devil's Advocate?" they asked.

"Oh, you just object to everything — challenge everything — disagree all around."

"That's for us," they said.

For a while, the meetings were held in a small office in Sacred Heart rectory. The group grew so rapidly that it moved to the parish library. This was a handy arrangement, because nearly always it was possible to find a book on the shelves to settle any argument.

Later, as the group began to divide and divide again, meetings were held in the homes or apartments of members. Mary and I and Bussie had moved into a new apartment not far from our old one, and we had a roomy living room. As meetings were held there, Mary became interested. Bussie was in her glory, because she was allowed to stay out of bed late, and to pass cheese and crackers during the social period which followed each discussion.

She was four years of age now, and there were no signs of an increase in the family. Mary and I talked it over several times, and finally I went to see Father Coakley.

"We want to adopt a baby," I told him.

He remarked that we were young. "You'll probably have lots of children of your own."

"We've waited long enough," I said firmly.

"Very well." He leaned back in his chair. "Joe, I've found

almost invariably that God sends children of their own to people who adopt a child."

"The more the merrier. We'd be happy to have a dozen. We've lost two. We're tired of that."

Father Coakley arranged for us to visit an orphanage, but apparently he did not make matters entirely clear to the Sisters in charge.

We waited for a little while in the orphanage parlor, and then were taken in tow by a smiling nun. From floor to floor we went, our hearts going out to the little ones in their cribs.

Back in the parlor, we sat down, and I said to Mary, "Did you pick one, or will you take anyone you can get?"

The nun looked slightly alarmed. "Did you come here with the idea of adopting a child?"

"Why else?" I inquired.

She fluttered her hands in embarrassment and sympathy. "But not one of these babies is available for adoption! Every one of them has a father or mother, or both, who expect to claim them later."

She promised to let us know if the situation changed. We went home somewhat disconcerted. Never had it occurred to us that there weren't hundreds of babies in need of adopted parents.

One day not long afterward, Bussie said to me firmly, "Dad, I want a baby brother."

I averted my eyes from hers. "Honey, I can't give you a baby brother. Nobody but God can do that."

"Then I'll tell God I want a baby brother."

"You do that. I'll help you pray."

She took my hand and tugged. "Come on."

"Come on where?"

"To church."

"All right — after dinner."

"No, Daddy — now!"

We walked the short distance to Sacred Heart Church and went inside. Bussie prayed energetically.

On the way home, I said cautiously, "You know, honey, you mustn't be disappointed if we don't get a baby . . . right soon, you know."

She looked up at me in astonishment. "I told God I wanted one, didn't I?"

"Yes, of course — ."

"Well!"

Never had I seen such faith.

A few months later, I told Father Coakley that we were going to become parents again. He slapped his hand hard on his desk and cried delightedly. "Didn't I tell you? When people adopt a baby, they get one of their own!"

"But we didn't adopt one."

"You had the good intention, and that's enough for God." Then Father Coakley repeated one of his favorite expressions: "God cannot be outdone in generosity."

After a little silence, I said to him, "You know, Father, I'm pretty nervous about this business. We've lost two children — and Mary didn't have an easy time. I'd like to take her to a good obstetrician."

With his Gatling-gun rapidity of speech, he said, "I'll send you to the best obstetrician on earth."

I shook my head. "I can't afford one *that* good."

He scribbled a note and handed it to me. "You take that note, and you and Mary go to him and tell him I sent you."

The obstetrician read Father Coakley's note, smiled, and said, "Fine."

Horribly embarrassed, I mentioned to him that I had no income except my limited salary.

"I'd better explain myself," he said. "I'm not in business. I have certain skills and talents which do not belong to me. They belong to God and to people who need my help. I've got to have a certain amount of money to pay my rent, my nurse, and so on. And I've got to support my own family. My well-to-do clients pay well for my services. My really poor clients pay nothing. You'll pay only what you can comfortably afford. Now — will you stop worrying and let me take care of everything?"

Each day, Bussie and I had been going to church as soon as I got home from work to pray for a baby brother. Now I was to discover that Bussie had the normal touch of feminine changeableness. As we knelt together one late afternoon, she leaned to me and whispered, "Daddy, I'm telling God I changed my mind. I want a sister instead of a brother. Mother and I decided that a sister would be nicer."

My face must have fallen slightly, because she added soothingly, "You can pray for a baby brother, Daddy. That will be all right."

I knew from her tone that although she felt that it would be all right, she was also sure that it would be useless. I agreed with her. There was not much use in pitting my puny prayers against her innocently pressing petitions.

It was a strangely comforting experience to have the obstetrician come to me in the room where I waited in the hospital, take my hand in a firm grip, and tell me that everything was fine — "you have a nice baby daughter."

Dawn was breaking when I went from Mary's bedside to the nursery to peer through the window at our new child. She was not at all as Mary had been. She was not jaundiced, she was not scowling, and one eye was not open to glare accusingly at me. She was a pretty pink and white infant with a round head and delicate features.

I got into the Ford and rode away from the hospital through a drizzling rain. I stopped in Sacred Heart Church to voice my gratitude at 6 o'clock Mass. My joy was inexpressible.

After Mass, I went home and foolishly wakened Bussie from a sound sleep to tell her, "You have a baby sister, honey. A beautiful baby sister." Womanlike, she wept inconsolably. The good news had come too suddenly for her.

We named our pink and white little one Elizabeth Ann Seton, in honor of Mother Seton, foundress of the Sisters of Charity, of which my sister was a member.

Not long before Betty's birth, Father Coakley had given me a story for the *Sun-Telegraph* about the baptismal font that was being made for Sacred Heart Church. It was to be the first baptismal font in the history of Christianity with an electrical heating element to warm the water.

Father Coakley said to me, while I scribbled notes, "Joe, ever since I was a young curate, I have resented the necessity of pouring cold water on the heads of tiny infants. I made up my mind that if ever I became a pastor, the baptismal water would be scientifically heated to exactly the right temperature — body temperature. That's what the new Sacred Heart font will do."

I hastened now to tell him about the birth of Betty. He sat forward in his chair in his high-strung, energetic way, pointed a slender forefinger at me, and said, "All right. All right, Joe Breig. You go to the hospital and tell your wife that your baby will be the first baby in the two thousand year history of the Church to be baptized with electrically warmed water."

Father Carroll baptized Betty. I knew he had an enormous aversion to being photographed. Nevertheless, I had a photographer from the *Sun-Telegraph* present when the time for the baptism came.

Father Carroll protested. I put my arm across his shoulders for a moment and said, "Now look, Father; why don't you attend to your baptizing, and let us newspapermen earn our livings?"

He grinned and made no more objections. We photographed Betty as she became the world's first warm-water Christian.

11

About this time there came into our lives two extraordinary personalities. One was Jim Flannery, the other William Queen.

I first met Jim when I went one evening to St. Joseph House of Hospitality, in Pittsburgh's Hill District, to get a feature story for the *Sun-Telegraph*.

St. Joseph House was in an abandoned school building in a Negro area. It had been turned into a refuge for homeless and jobless men by Father Charles Owen Rice, Pittsburgh's best-known "labor priest."

Father Rice had organized what he called — with considerable daring — the Catholic Radical Alliance. The *Sun-Telegraph's* editors wondered what it was all about, and assigned me to find out.

Father Rice had chosen the word "radical" after much thought. He said he wanted to attract attention to his movement — and he succeeded in that. Furthermore, he wanted to restore to the word "radical" its root meaning (no pun intended) of "going to the roots of things." Father Rice wanted his alliance to inspire people to get at the roots of social evils, to study them, and to take the proper steps to correct them.

The House of Hospitality, of course, owed much of its

inspiration to Dorothy Day and Peter Maurin, who had opened, on Mott Street in New York, the first Catholic Worker House of Hospitality.

I drove up steep Wiley Avenue through the darkness, and after some inquiries found Tannehill Street and parked in front of St. Joseph House. It was a gaunt, draughty, forbidding structure, approached by a flight of concrete steps. As I mounted them, I nearly fell over a couple of men lolling in the warm night air. "Gimme a cig, Bud," said one.

I handed out cigarettes and went inside. I found myself in a dimly lighted, empty corridor.

Rather, it appeared empty. Groping around, I came upon a couple more men, seated on a stairway that led to the second floor. Again I passed out cigarettes, and was directed to a room where I would find Father Rice.

Perhaps a dozen onlookers listened while I interviewed the young priest. I met them all, and among them was Flannery. He was the youngest, and he attracted me. We fell into conversation, and because I wanted to know him better, I suggested that he come to a meeting of the Sheep and Goats some evening.

A few weeks later, he did so. He became a faithful member of the group, and we began to be fast friends.

Gradually, I learned Flannery's story, and his hopes and dreams. He was an orphan. He had left his home in Brooklyn to travel with a road show as a scene-shifter. The show folded up in Wheeling, West Virginia, and Flannery, with a few dollars in his pocket, set out to hitchhike to Pittsburgh. He reasoned that there ought to be work for him in "the workshop of the world."

There wasn't. Day after day he walked the streets of Pittsburgh, growing hungrier and hungrier, and sleeping on park benches. He was too embarrassed to beg, although once he did stop a prosperous-looking man to ask for a meal. The man fed him well, but soon Flannery was hungry again.

At last he wandered into the Hill District, saw a church open, went inside and into the confessional, and said to the startled priest, "Father, I'm starving." He was told either to go to the rectory or to walk the few blocks to St. Joseph House. He chose the latter.

The hospitality houses at that time were doing a magnificent work of mercy in precisely such emergencies. A man could go in at any time of day or night, without introduction or credentials, and be fed and housed. No one asked questions; no one demanded that the visitors proclaim "conversion" or "walk the sawdust." Flannery was so impressed with this charity that he decided to stay and devote himself to the work.

Into St. Joseph House not long afterward came William Queen — although he was not then known by that name. He was universally called "Bro." He had been a religious Brother, but had become so fascinated by the Houses of Hospitality that he had been released to go into that field.

He was then a plump little man, but before long became a very thin little man because of the austerities of the life. One thing about him, however, never changed — his short, barking laugh.

During this period, Mary and I decided that, considering the amount of rent we were paying, we could buy a house. We prayed to St. Anthony for guidance, and telephoned to the real estate people.

One day an agent picked us up in his auto and drove through the Liberty Tubes and up the long hill into Brook-

line. The auto crested still another hill and stopped in front
of a roomy brick bungalow with a big yard around it. We
walked up the concrete steps, went through the house, and
asked the agent the price. When he told us, my face fell.

"We can't pay nearly that much," I said.

"Make an offer," he suggested.

"The offer I'd make," I replied disconsolately, "would
be an insult."

The agent smiled. "Let me tell you something," he said.
"You can't insult anybody by offering good honest dollars.
You tell me what you think you can pay, and I'll transmit
the offer to the owner."

I did so. A period of dickering followed, during which I
was counseled by a builder — the father of one of the young
women in the Sheep and Goats. "Don't sit tight on your
offer," he advised. "Go up a hundred dollars or so every time
the owner comes down. You want the house — go after it. I
think you'll get it at a price within your means."

He was right. One day my offers and the counteroffers
coincided. I borrowed all I could on my insurance, and Mary
and I met the owner in the real estate office. My hand trem-
bled so much that I could hardly sign the check for the down
payment, but at last the house was ours.

Not long after we moved in, Flannery telephoned. "Bro
and I have decided to open a new House of Hospitality on
the South Side," he said. "I'd like to talk to you about it."

Thus was initiated the odd partnership between St. Francis House of Hospitality and our house in Brookline, which
we soon enough dubbed St. Anthony House.

"St. Anthony House" became a refuge for Flannery and Bro
and some of the other men who helped to operate St. Francis

House. When one of them grew exhausted from lack of sleep, irregular meals, and struggles with cockroaches and bedbugs, he came to our house for a few days to recuperate.

There is a legend in our family about our "bedbug miracle." One warm night, I looked up from where I was seated, reading, in the living room, to see our front door opening and Bro sidling through. "Hi," he said.

I returned his greeting. He closed the door, turned, and went through a mysterious series of maneuvers.

He took off his coat and made as if to drop it on the daven-port. With his arm outstretched, he paused, shook his head, walked to an overstuffed chair, and again extended his hand, holding the coat. Again he shook his head and turned away, still holding the coat in front of him.

"Bro," I inquired, "have you gone mad?"

He uttered his short, barking laugh, and this time dropped the coat on a chair. "No madder than usual, but I'm buggy, and I was thinking of Mary." He made a sweeping gesture. "But of course she's not afraid of bedbugs."

I leaped up. "Oh, isn't she, though!" I seized the coat — a disreputable thing — carried it into the back yard, and dumped it into the garbage can. I returned and shepherded Bro upstairs to the bathroom. "Get in there and take a bath," I ordered, "and throw everything you're wearing out the back window."

He protested feebly. "But I've no other clothes!"

"Never mind that," I interrupted. "Get in there and undress and throw out everything."

I stood in the back yard, assembled the garments gingerly as they came fluttering down, and consigned them to the garbage. Then I returned to the house and called Mary, and together we went through wardrobes and drawers, collecting an outfit for Bro. I handed it into the bathroom to him and resumed my seat in the living room.

Presently, down came Bro, clad in many colors and in trousers too large for him, but clean and bugless. "I didn't know you worried about bedbugs," he said sheepishly. Mary threw up her hands.

That night, before I went to bed, I knelt and made a pact with St. Francis. I told him that his helpers from St. Francis House were welcome in our house at any time — but the bedbugs weren't. I suggested that he take care of the problem.

For five years thereafter, the men from St. Francis House came and went, eating and sleeping with us, and never did they leave a bedbug behind.

Among them was a man — call him Harry — who was intimately acquainted with hobo jungles in states from the Gulf of Mexico to the Canadian border. At the most unexpected moments, he appeared to sit down to dinner with us and to spend an evening. Then he would depart as suddenly as he had come.

One evening, after we had had one of those sieges of sickness which sometimes afflict a family, Harry and I were having a snack in the kitchen. I growled something about being hard up for money.

He stared at me. "I thought you had lots of money!" he exclaimed.

I laughed hollowly.

He began to reach into pocket after pocket and to pile pennies, nickels, dimes, quarters, and half dollars on the kitchen table. I watched openmouthed. "Will this help?" he asked.

"Harry," I said helplessly, "I don't want your money. Don't take my grousing so seriously."

"Look," he said, "if this isn't enough, I've got a few hundred in the bank."

"I thought you were —." I stopped.

"A hobo? Sure — but I manage to keep a few dollars stowed away."

He must have sensed my curiosity, because he went on, "You see, any time I'm walking along the street — like when I'm on the way to the streetcar to come to visit you — I take up a little collection."

"Collection?"

"Yes. For my favorite charity."

"What's that?"

"Buying crutches for crippled centipedes."

I shook my head. "I don't understand, Harry."

He leaned toward me, earnestly. "Look, I stop people in the street, and I say, 'Would you like to make a little donation to my favorite charity?' When they ask me, 'What's that?' I tell them, 'Buying crutches for crippled centipedes.' That makes them laugh — puts them in a good humor — and they hand me a nickel or dime or quarter. That's all there is to it."

He grinned like a delighted boy.

I chuckled, but pushed his money back to him. "Really, Harry, thanks a lot, but we're all right. You'll need it for your crippled centipedes."

He shoveled the money back into his pockets, shaking his head dolefully at the idea of anybody refusing a loan.

One Sunday the phone rang. I answered and heard the voice of our city editor, Alex Zehner. "Can you come to the office, Joe? The Germans and Russians have invaded Poland."

The lights had begun going out, not only all over Europe, but in millions of hearts all over the world.

Flannery was scandalized by the weird partnership between the United States and Soviet Russia. He signed for the draft, but when he was called up, he told the draft board his conscience would not let him go.

"I can't fight for godless communism," he said.

No amount of argument swayed him. He had session after session with a sympathetic and weary draft board which declined to expose him to prosecution and felt that sooner or later he would see the matter in a different light.

The day after Pearl Harbor, he was waiting when the draft board's office opened. "Now my conscience is clear," he said. "Our country has been attacked."

The draft board chairman held his head. "You've got the record so fouled up," he said, "that maybe they won't even let you into the army now."

But they did. One night we rode to Union Station with Flannery to see him off. All the way, he clung to Bussie as if he could not let her go.

"You're what I'll be fighting for, honey," he said over and over. "You and the other kids. I want to remember you in my arms. That's the only thing that will ever help me to make sense out of this thing. That's the only thing that will keep me going."

She stared at him, puzzled.

Union Station was a mass of milling, tearful fathers and mothers, brothers and sisters, uncles and aunts and cousins. We stood against the barricade and waved to Flannery until he disappeared into a coach. Then we rode home in silence.

We were not to see Flannery for four years. He was sent almost at once to the Pacific, and fought his way as a combat infantryman all the way from the Solomons to Japan.

12

It was a Sunday afternoon in spring. Heavy rain was falling. Our doorbell rang. Mary opened, and called to me in a shocked voice.

Standing on our porch, his hatless head hunched into his shoulders, his hands thrust deep in the pockets of a tattered overcoat, was the short, drenched, bedraggled figure of Johnny the alcoholic.

Naturally Mary was startled. She had never seen Johnny before, and he was an alarming, pitiable sight. Everybody at the *Sun-Telegraph* knew him. He haunted the alley beside the building, slept in any corner from which he was not ejected, and cadged dimes and quarters for drinks from good-humored newspapermen.

He looked at me now with tragic, pleading eyes. "Get me into a hospital, Joe. I'm going into the rams." His body was shaking convulsively.

I had never heard that particular expression, "the rams." Later Johnny was to describe the experience vividly to me. I gathered that the mind of the victim becomes separated from reality, and enters into a nightmare world of horrifying hallucinations.

I could see now that Johnny was terrified. He took a shaking hand out of his overcoat pocket and seized my arm.

"You've got to get me into a hospital, Joe. You've got to."

I led him into the living room and got him out of his overcoat. He was wet through and through.

I asked Mary to bring a couple of blankets. While she was gone, I got Johnny undressed and wrapped him in a cover from the brown couch where so many men from St. Francis House of Hospitality had slept.

I got towels and helped him to dry himself. He kept talking wildly about a hospital and the rams. Mary brought blankets and hot coffee, and presently Johnny put his head down on the couch and fell into an uneasy, trembling doze.

I went into the kitchen and explained Johnny to Mary. "Don't be afraid of him," I told her. "He's a gentle soul. He just won't stay away from liquor; and it's poison to him."

"What if he dies here, Joe?"

I grinned at her. "Johnny won't die. He's got a tough little body."

"What are we going to do with him?"

"Let him sleep for a while. Maybe he'll snap out of this. If he doesn't, we'll see about getting him into a hospital."

I went into the living room and stood looking down at Johnny's haggard, lined face as he slept. He was a young man, but he had the curiously old and worn look that comes of dissipation, lack of sleep, insufficient nourishment, and ceaseless weariness.

I knew Johnny. I knew there was no trace of wickedness in him. In many ways, he was as innocent and guileless as a boy. I doubted that he had ever entertained a derogatory thought about anybody. And you never heard Johnny say anything that could not have been said in the hearing of his own mother. The cleanliness of his speech bespoke the essential cleanliness of his character.

I stood looking at him for a while. Then I went out of the living room, came back with a bottle of holy water, and sprinkled Johnny with it, saying a prayer for him as I did so.

An hour or two later, he wakened. Now he was able to speak more calmly and rationally, without the wild urgency of his first words. Some of the terror was gone from his eyes.

He told me of a hospital in Pittsburgh where they specialized in cases like his. "Get me in, Joe," he begged.

"I'm willing to try, Johnny. But if I get you in, then what? They'll straighten you up, and the minute they release you, you'll be back on the bottle again."

"No, Joe — not this time."

"You know, Johnny, you can't just go on this way. Some night you'll die of exposure, or walk in front of a truck, or something. This isn't what God made you for."

"I know, Joe. I'm finished. It's going to be different from now on."

I helped him to get back into his dried clothing. We drove to the hospital. I signed him in and left him there.

A few days later, he telephoned. He was ready to be released, but he didn't trust himself. And he had no money, of course, to pay for the care he had received. Would I come and get him out, and stay with him for a few hours so that he wouldn't go straight to a saloon?

I went around among the fellows at the *Sun-Telegraph* and took up a collection to pay Johnny's bill. At the hospital, I found him clean and bright-eyed, no longer shaking. He was a very likable little chap now.

I brought him home, and for a week did not let him out of my sight. He slept on the brown couch, and went to work with me each morning.

I explained the situation to City Editor Zehner, and he told me, "Just stick with him all the time. That's your assignment until you get him straightened out."

Johnny was restless. He was burning with a feverish energy. I suppose his nerves were clamoring for a drink. Every evening he insisted that we go for a walk. We trudged miles and miles, his short legs pumping away at a pace that hurried me to keep up with him. Thousands of words poured out of him. And he drank buttermilk constantly.

I did not dare to so much as open a bottle of beer in his presence. I drank buttermilk with him until I hated the sight of it.

Mary and the children grew very fond of Johnny. Strangely enough, so did Mary's Aunt Annie, who was visiting us at the time, and had been scandalized at first over the presence of this disreputable creature in our house.

One evening he told us, "I'm going to try to get into the army. I think that ought to straighten me out."

It seemed like a good idea. I went with him to the recruiting offices, and one day we said good-by to him as he went away spick and span in his new uniform.

Some months later, I went out for lunch and was crossing the alley beside the *Sun-Telegraph* on my way to a restaurant when Johnny accosted me. He was in civvies, he had been drinking, and he was dirty and wild-eyed again.

He asked for a quarter.

For the first time, I refused. "I'll not give you a cent," I said.

Johnny was shocked. He stared at my angry face. "Joe, aren't we friends any more?" he whined.

"I'm your friend, Johnny, and that's why I'll give you nothing. You got kicked out of the army, didn't you?"

He hung his head.

"For drinking, eh?"

He avoided my eyes.

I gave him a tongue-lashing. "The fellows at the *Sun-Tele* chipped in to give you a new start. Most of those fellows have families. They need their money. You've gone back on them. You've gone back on the army. You just don't want to do right, Johnny. You want to do what you want to do. You won't try. You're a quitter. I'm your friend, but I don't like this, Johnny. Good-by."

I walked away, leaving him staring piteously after me.

My outburst proved providential. Johnny was profoundly shamed. The next time I saw him, he was neatly dressed, his hair was combed, his face and hands clean.

"I've got a job, Joe. I'm working every day."

I showed no enthusiasm. "How long will you keep it up?"

He held up his right hand. "From now on, Joe. I'm not going back on you and Mary and Alex Zehner and the others again."

I shook hands with him, but I warned, "You'll have to prove it, Johnny."

"I'll prove it, all right."

"I hope you do."

He did. Many years have passed since that time, and although I have not seen Johnny, I receive post cards and letters from him. He is still working, and he has not touched liquor. I salute him. So does Mary.

13

THE WAR YEARS were long years. We worried over Jim Flannery as if he were a son or a brother. Bussie and I went often to church to pray for him. Now and then we received a letter from him, but he was exasperatingly uncommunicative about himself.

He talked about poetry, or books, or the Virgin Mary, to whom he was profoundly devoted. Once he mentioned the beauty of a lagoon fringed with tropical trees in the moonlight; from which we deduced that he was fighting the island to island war with MacArthur. This only increased our anxiety, although in a way it was comforting to have some clue to his whereabouts. Before that, we had almost the feeling that he had vanished into some disembodied state apart from our universe.

A box we sent one Christmas contained a curious conglomeration of odds and ends. Mary and Bussie and I conferred at length on this and that suggestion, trying to decide what would be most useful to include in the limited package we were permitted to mail. We hailed with delight the thought that we should put in some candles; surely a man in a combat area would find them serviceable. And I remember vividly a little tin triangle, four or five inches high, which had been painted to resemble a Christmas tree and punctured with holes, so that a lighted candle might be placed behind it to shine through.

Just before we closed the box and wrapped it in heavy paper, Bussie came running with a final gift — a tiny crib, and tiny images of the Infant Jesus, of Mary, and of Joseph.

Months later, we heard from Flannery. He wrote that for Christmas a year previous, he and his buddies had suspended oranges, bits of candy, and some greenery from an open umbrella, and called it their Christmas tree.

"You have no idea what your box meant to us," he wrote. "This Christmas, we had your tin Christmas tree, and the Nativity scene. We set up the crèche in front of the tree, lighted a candle behind it, and sat there feasting our eyes on the light shining through the holes. It was wonderful."

By this time, we had organized a study club in our new parish. It met always in our "St. Anthony House," because Mary was not well, and anyhow baby-sitters were scarce.

One night somebody came with a two-inch newspaper clipping which said that Pope Pius XII, in a radio broadcast to Portugal, had consecrated the world to the Immaculate Heart of Mary, as requested by Our Lady of Fatima. The story mentioned, in passing, that our Lady, appearing near a village called Fatima, in Portugal, in 1917, had outlined to three shepherd children a spiritual program which would bring from God the blessing of peace.

We were scandalized. Twenty-five years had passed since 1917! If our Lady had appeared to point us the way to peace, why had the world not heard about her message? We agreed that we would make it our business to find out about the events of Fatima, and to publicize them.

Nobody, however, seemed to know anything about Fatima. Persons to whom we put our inquiries grinned embarrassedly and said the word meant nothing to them but a brand of cigarettes.

Finally, one night, Bro came to our weekly meeting with a leaflet he had found in the pamphlet rack of an obscure South Side church. We wrote to the publisher, were referred to the Benedictine Sisters of Perpetual Adoration at Clyde, Missouri, and at last obtained from them a pamphlet containing the story of the apparitions at Fatima. They also put us on the track of an inexpensive, but reasonably complete leaflet published in Chicago.

For months thereafter, visitors to our home were as likely as not to find us seated around the dining-room table, folding leaflets and addressing envelopes. We mailed thousands of leaflets to anybody who would promise to distribute them. And we sent some to Flannery.

Meanwhile, I was soliciting invitations to speak to club meetings and Communion breakfasts in the Pittsburgh area, so that I could tell people about Fatima.

A letter from Flannery gave me the perfect climax for my talks. As one of the conditions for peace, our Lady at Fatima had asked people to receive Communion on the first Saturday of each month in reparation for the sins of mankind, and to recite the Rosary while meditating with her on the mysteries of the Redemption.

Flannery's letter informed us that on the first "First Saturday" after he had received the leaflets, a dozen or more fighting men rose with him at 4 a.m. to hike fifteen miles to a place where they could go to Mass and receive Communion.

Fortunately, an army truck came along after they had

walked a few miles. He described vividly the ride through the tropical dawn, the men praying the Rosary and singing hymns as they rode.

After that, I ended each of my talks on Fatima by reading Flannery's letter and asking my audience whether we could not walk a block or two to church for Mass on first Saturdays, seeing that the soldiers who were defending us were willing to set out on a fifteen-mile hike after rising long before reveille.

Apparently the time had come when, in God's providence, the message of Fatima was to become known far and wide. The news began bobbing up here and there, and more and more people began to spread the word.

But there was one little thing that was missing, and that would have jolted a lot of people, I think, into paying attention to the message. This was a shoe that had belonged to Flannery.

We came into possession of the shoe in this manner: once when Mary was in a hospital — for what reason I cannot now recall — Flannery came to visit her.

I found him chatting with her when I arrived after my day's work at the *Sun-Telegraph*. We talked gaily for a while, and for some reason I suddenly recalled something that Bro had said a few days before. He had remarked with a chuckle that Flannery had exchanged shoes with some poor man at St. Francis House, "and you ought to see what he got in the exchange!"

Now I looked at Flannery's shoes. They looked all right. Nevertheless, I commanded him, "Let me see your shoes."

He glanced down. "What's wrong with those shoes?"

"I want to see the soles."

He kept his feet planted firmly on the floor. I reached

down suddenly, seized his ankle, and yanked his foot up. What I saw was a bare foot through a great hole in the sole.

I pointed outside. "Snow on the ground, and you're walking around like that. You idiot — do you want to get pneumonia?"

"I'm healthy," he told me argumentatively.

"Listen," I said. "When you leave here, you're going to wear my overshoes. And you're going straight to our house. I'll meet you there later. I'll give you a pair of shoes. But there'll be a condition attached to them — you can't give them away. Promise?"

Reluctantly, he did so.

For a long time afterward — even after Flannery had gone into the army — the shoes with the big holes in the soles were around the house.

When we received Flannery's letter about the early-morning trip to a battle-front chapel for first-Saturday Communion, I said to Mary, "Where are those shoes of Flannery's? I'll take one of them along when I make speeches about Our Lady of Fatima. I'll tell the story of the shoes. Then I'll read Flannery's letter. And I'll wind up the talk saying, 'And here, ladies and gentlemen, is one of those shoes.' I'll hold it up and put my hand through the hole in the sole, and wiggle my fingers. It'll floor 'em!"

And it would have floored them — but we couldn't find the shoes. The woman who came occasionally to clean house for us had thrown them out. She didn't know what a great cause she was hampering.

Another extraordinary visitor to our "St. Anthony House" was Father Patrick Peyton.

I had never heard of Father Peyton until I received a

long-distance telephone call from Tom Byrne in Cleveland, who had been a classmate at Notre Dame. "Joe," he said, "there's a young priest who's going to call on you one of these days. His name is Father Pat Peyton. He wants to get ten million Americans to promise to recite the Rosary every day in their homes."

I thought I wasn't hearing correctly. "How many Americans?"

"Ten million."

"How's he going about it, Tom?"

"Well, he's been sending out some letters, and making a few speeches."

I paused. "Look, Tom — you know as well as I do that you can't reach ten million Americans that way. This is a big country."

"Well, that's just the point, Joe. This young fellow isn't long over from Ireland. He doesn't know the problems of reaching the American people with a message. That's why I told him to come to you. You're a newspaperman. Maybe you can give him some ideas."

"Well, anyhow," I said, "I'll tell him about Our Lady of Fatima."

Tom laughed his big laugh. "I warned him you'd do that, Joe."

One early evening, Father Peyton loomed in our doorway. He seemed to fill it with his broad stooping shoulders and his six feet four inches in height.

"Glory be to God," said Father Peyton. "Ah, but it's good to see you!" He had a brogue as broad as a stage Irishman's.

We listened fascinated while he poured out his story, first in the living room, then at the dining-room table right through dinner, and then in the living room again. Never had we met anybody so consumed with zeal and so possessed of a bottomless sincerity. It was a scandal to him that Catholic families were not praying the Rosary together each evening in their homes. He was horrified, he was crushed, he was hurt at this neglect. He was determined that it should be rectified, at no matter what cost to him.

He told us how, in his boyhood in Ireland, he had thought of being a priest. Then, as he grew into adolescence and young manhood, he would stand in the potato patch, leaning on his hoe, dreaming about America.

"I was a materialist, I was," he said. "My parents wanted me to be a priest. But I stood in that potato patch thinking about the glamor of America, longing to see the bright lights of this country. I was nineteen years old, and I told my old father and mother I was going across the Atlantic.

"Every night as long as I could remember, we had knelt in our little cottage, the whole family of us, praying the Rosary together. Ah! What an example that father and mother set for us! The first sounds we heard in our infancy were the prayers of the Rosary. But in spite of it all, I grew up to be a materialist, dreaming of glamor, seeing bright lights in my imagination while I stood in the potato patch."

We could not forebear to smile as we listened to this confession torn from the soul of this boyish young man with the broad Irish face.

After he came to America, Father Peyton worked as a slate-picker in the coal mines. Then he took a job at the cathedral. One day he was painting in the sacristy, and suddenly he put down the brush, hunted up the pastor, and said, "I'm going to be a priest, as I should be."

He was sent to the seminary of the Holy Cross Fathers at the University of Notre Dame, and one day he started spitting blood. He concealed his illness for a long time, but at last there came a gush of bright red blood into his mouth. At the hospital, he was told that his tuberculosis was so far advanced that the doctors would have to remove a couple of ribs and collapse the affected lung. His condition was complicated by adhesions.

A few days before the scheduled operation, he was visited by a priest. "Pat," said the visitor, "I wouldn't consent to this operation. Why don't you ask our Lady to make you well?"

"I *have* asked her," replied the young seminarian. "I've asked her, and I guess the operation is her answer. That's the way I'm to be made well."

"Nonsense," the priest told him. "She can do better than that for you. Look, Pat — she's a woman, and women love to be talked to. Talk to her, man — talk to her!"

Patrick Peyton "talked to her," and soon afterward felt so well that new X rays were taken. His lung had healed. There was no operation.

At the time of his ordination, Father Peyton told us, he sat for a long time, thinking and praying. He had determined that in gratitude for his cure, he would dedicate his whole life to the service of our Lady. What should he do?

It came to him that he would crusade, as long as he had breath in his body, for the daily Family Rosary in every home. In a great burst of daring, he selected as his goal "ten million Americans praying the Rosary every blessed day of their lives."

So there he was, seated in our living room, looking to us for suggestions.

We kicked the problem around for a while, and finally I said, "Look, Father, do you realize that the thirty-or-so-million American Catholics are scattered across a country three thousand miles wide? This isn't Ireland."

He looked at me helplessly.

"You can't reach an audience like that by going around making speeches," I told him. "It would take you a couple dozen lifetimes. And you can't do it by mail. Too expensive."

"I've got to do it," he said. "I want to know how. Tom Byrne thought maybe you could tell me how."

"When a big company wants to sell something in America," I remarked, half in soliloquy, "or when some organization wants to put over an idea, they get the movie stars to endorse it. Movie stars are the idols of Americans."

I grinned. "It would be a wonderful thing to get the idols to help you bring people closer to God, wouldn't it?"

Father Peyton's face bore an expression of desperation. "But I'm a poor unknown young priest. How can I get these great movie people to help me tell people about the Family Rosary? Why should they listen to me?"

I answered confidently. "Father Peyton, I've been covering City Hall here in Pittsburgh for a couple of years. I've been a newspaperman for fourteen years. I have learned one thing for sure."

Emphasizing my words, I said, "Important people are easy to approach, and willing to help. Americans are goodhearted and generous. And they have a great, great respect for priests. I think you ought to go to Hollywood some day, and tell your story there."

Two or three years later, Father Peyton told me an odd story. Somebody had telephoned and left a message for him:

the plane reservation to Los Angeles, for which he had asked, was ready for him. Apparently he had mentioned to somebody his desire to go to Hollywood, and then had forgotten it.

He debated with himself for a while, and finally boarded the plane. He landed in Los Angeles and walked to a taxi. The taximan threw down his flag, and inquired, "Where to, Father?"

"I don't know," said Father Peyton, with that distressed expression that comes upon his face when he is uncertain what to do next. At such moments, he looks as helpless as a baby.

The driver waited patiently. Presently Father Peyton said, "Just take me to the nearest church."

The taximan either disobeyed, or he didn't know where the nearest church was. He passed it and drew up in front of the Church of the Good Shepherd — the parish church of many world-famed movie stars.

Father Peyton paid the taximan, went into the church, and knelt to pray. Here he was, in a great city on the west coast of this great, glamorous, frightening America — and he didn't know a soul. He had come to win Hollywood to his cause, and he hadn't so much as a letter of introduction to anybody.

While he knelt there, the pastor came along the aisle and said to him, "Can I help you, Father?"

Father Peyton went into the back of the church and poured his story into a sympathetic ear. The following Sunday, he preached at all the Masses, telling with his touching fervor his story of dedicating his life to our Lady, and of promising to persuade ten million Americans to say the Rosary every blessed day of their lives.

"I'll be waitin' in the sacristy after each Mass," he said,

"and if there are any of you great movie stars who will do a favor for our Lady, come to me there and tell me."

They came — Bing Crosby, Ethel Barrymore, Loretta Young, Irene Dunne, and the rest. Within a week or so, Father Peyton was one of the best-known personages in Hollywood. Dozens of actors and actresses pledged themselves to donate their talents to a radio program which would publicize family prayer.

The result was the network radio program, "Family Theater," which made Father Peyton's name known not only all over America, but even abroad, and made a household word out of his slogan, "The family that prays together, stays together."

Father Peyton was launched on a career that was to carry him to England, across Europe, to Australia and New Zealand, and into Africa, India, Burma, Pakistan, Ceylon —. Everywhere.

He has not changed, except that his sandy hair has grayed, and he has grown heavier. Years later, he grinned like a boy when I remarked, "Father Peyton, do you remember the potato patch in Ireland, and how you leaned on your hoe dreaming of the glamor of America, and decided that you'd rather have the glamor than be a priest? And where did you land? On a slag pile in Scranton! Then you *did* become a priest, and where did you go? To Hollywood to meet all the glamorous people you had heard about. You see, God was willing to let you have the glamor — if you would use it in His service."

"Go away with you, Joe Breig," said Father Peyton.

14

Now THE TIME HAD COME when we were to be given a son to ease the pain of the loss of our first-born. Why I was sure in advance that the new baby would be a boy, I do not know. The obstetrician said that all the signs indicated another girl, but I smiled and said, "This one's a boy; you can bank on that."

Mary, for the first time, was profoundly troubled about the approaching confinement. "Something's wrong, Joe," she told me more than once. "I'm afraid the baby's not going to live."

A few years before, her fears would have alarmed me. Now they did not. "Everything's going to be fine," I assured her. "You wait and see."

Because of the war-caused shortage of nurses, I was allowed to be with my wife until the last moment in the hospital. The time came suddenly, and excited nurses began wheeling the bed swiftly along a corridor. I walked alongside, holding Mary's hand. At the elevator, there was a little delay.

Mary turned her face up from the pillow and said softly, "Joe." I leaned over so that she could whisper to me.

"Joe, I know I'm not coming back. The baby and I are going to die." Never had she talked like that before.

I put my hand on her cheek and said, "Listen, Mary. Believe me. You know how hard we've tried to make Our Lady of Fatima known. Do you think she doesn't appreciate that? I tell you, I know she's going to take care of you. You'll be back soon with a wonderful baby son. I'm not guessing; I know it."

She smiled uncertainly and was whisked away from me into the elevator.

Not long afterward, the physician whom Father Coakley had called "the greatest obstetrician on earth" came to me with a great smile, holding out both hands. "Here," he exclaimed, "I want to shake hands with a *real* obstetrician. How in the world did you know this was going to be a boy?"

"Then it *is* a boy," I said.

"A magnificent boy. And your wife is just fine. You can go to her room and wait for her. She'll be there in a few minutes."

He gave me the number of the room, and I was waiting when Mary's bed was wheeled in. I sat waiting for her to awaken from the sleep induced by ether.

Presently she aroused enough to speak. "Joe — do we have a baby?"

"A beautiful boy," I told her. "And you're just fine."

She smiled and closed her eyes.

I waited.

Twenty or thirty minutes later, she wakened again, and again inquired, "Joe, do we have a baby?"

I leaned down and kissed her. "A boy — a nice boy, Mary. Don't you remember? I told you the first time you wakened."

"Honest, Joe? You're not kidding me?"

"Honey, don't I always tell you the truth? We've got a boy."

She dozed off again, only to waken later and repeat the same question. She could not believe the good news. At long last, I convinced her. Then she went back to sleep, and went on sleeping.

I went out of the room and asked a nurse to let me see my son. She led me to the nursery, stationed me at a window, went inside, lifted our boy from a crib, and brought him close.

I feasted my eyes on him. Our first son had looked like me; this one looked like Mary. My heart went out to him.

Presently I looked up at the nurse. She was smiling sympathetically. I smiled back, and formed with my lips the words, "Thank you." Then I went out of the hospital and reported for work — although I am afraid I spent most of the day telling people about our good fortune.

Next day, I went to the hospital with a young priest. I had discussed with our pastor my desire to baptize the baby immediately, not waiting until the time when Mary could leave the hospital. He had given his approval.

We found Mary sitting up in bed, looking well and cheerful. I told her that I had noticed that our son had been born on the day between the feasts of St. Paul and St. Anthony, the first Christian hermits. "So," said I, "I thought we'd name him Paul Anthony."

Mary said reproachfully, "Joe!"

"What's wrong with Paul Anthony?" I demanded.

"Nothing. But I want the name to be Joseph."

"I named the first boy Joseph when I baptized him," I argued.

"That doesn't matter. I want this one named Joseph, too."

"Everybody'll call him junior," I grumbled.

Mary smiled. "No. He won't be junior, because he'll not have your middle name."

I looked at her suspiciously. "You mean you've picked a middle name, too? Can't we name him Joseph Paul Anthony?"

She shook her head. "The nurse and I decided that he should be named Joseph Francis."

"The nurse! What's the nurse got to do with it? This isn't her kid!"

Mary took my hand. "She was nice to me, Joe. And it seemed just right when she suggested Francis. That's my father's name, and your father's middle name. It will please them both."

I stood looking helplessly at her, feeling much put upon.

The young priest had been enjoying the interchange immensely. Now he put his hand on my shoulder and said, "Joe, it's a woman's world. Let's baptize the baby Joseph Francis."

But I thought of those magnificent old desert hermits. I would not let them down. I squared my jaw. "All right," I said, "this one's Joseph Francis. But if we ever have another son, Mary, will you name him Paul Anthony? Or Anthony Paul? I've got a promise to those hermits to keep."

"All right, Joe," she said.

A nurse came into the room with our son, and a few minutes later he was a Christian.

Just after the water was poured and the words spoken, the nurse in charge of the floor came bustling in, much annoyed. "What's this all about?" she cried. "Why were you in such a hurry to baptize this baby? There's not a thing wrong with him."

The young priest grinned. "Nothing except that he's got a nervous father," he said, and sidled out of the room.

The nurse flounced away before I had a chance to explain to her that two of our babies had died, and therefore I might be excused for being apprehensive about delaying baptism.

I shrugged and turned back to Mary. The nurse holding our little Christian smiled and took him back to the nursery. Thenceforward — until he grew too tall for such a diminutive — he was to be known as Joey, in order to avoid the confusion of two Joes in the house.

I think of certain scenes in connection with Joey. One of the most vivid carries me again into a hospital.

Bussie, Betty, and Joe, all three, had contracted ear infections. Bussie was gravely ill, and the doctors advised separating the two others so that they would not cross-infect each other.

I see Mary and me handing Joey, at the age of ten months, to a nurse, and resigning ourselves to stay away from him for at least a fortnight, until his infection could be overcome.

We were advised not to visit him because he would want to come home. If he did not see us, he would be contented in the hospital.

Unable to bear the separation, we returned once or twice to steal a glimpse of him, being careful not to let him see us.

A nurse reconnoitered, and then beckoned to us. We peered through a half-opened door and saw Joey, seated in a little high chair, being fed by a tiny Sister who seemed hardly larger than he.

He appeared entirely happy, and we went away no

longer troubled by thoughts that he might be crying for us night and day.

I see us, at the end of the fortnight, going to the hospital again, this time to bring Joey home. There was an unaccountable series of delays. Everybody seemed to be taking turns making excuses for not producing Joey.

We understood when at last a nurse came along a corridor, holding our son in her arms. She was accompanied by half a dozen other nurses who were talking to the little one, touching his hands, begging him to give them a smile.

The nurse who held him stood for a long time talking with us, and seemed not to notice when Mary, once or twice, held out her arms to Joey. The other nurses clustered around, looking worshipfully at him.

We realized then that the hearts of nurses must bear the scars of a thousand wounds of separation. These young women could not endure parting from Joey. At long last, though, the nurse holding him thrust him into my wife's arms. "Please bring him back to see us," she begged.

They followed us to the elevator and peered through the narrowing gap until the closing door shut them out.

We rode half the way home in silence. I stole glances at Joey as he lay in his mother's arms, staring at her with solemn eyes.

"I believe he's forgotten who we are," I said.

"I've been thinking the same thing," said Mary. "He looks frightened, doesn't he?"

There was a silence, and then, "Those nurses," I said and sighed.

"I hated to take him away from them, Joe."

"So did I."

The bewildered expression on Joey's face persisted until we walked into our house and Betty came running forward, crying, "Joey! Joey!"

His eyes lighted and he flung himself toward Betty so suddenly that Mary nearly dropped him. Joey knew now that he was at home. He had forgotten his parents, but not the sister who had hardly left his side for a waking hour from the time of his earliest infancy.

I remember that the sides of Joey's crib were grimy from the clutch of Betty's hands as she stood each day looking at him sleeping, waiting for him to waken so that she could play with him and guard him as he crawled about the floor.

Sometimes I wished that we could keep the crib just as it was, with the prints of Betty's hands on its wooden bars. Devotion such as hers, I felt, ought to have its little monument, even though it could not be immortalized, as it deserved, in soaring spires and stately columns and arches.

Eventually, of course, the crib was cleaned and repainted, and used for the next child, and the next after that. Then we gave it away for the use of other infants, and for all we know it is doing duty to this day.

Joey's return from the hospital and his greeting of Betty closed what had been a terrifying period for us. It began one evening when a physician, hastily summoned to examine Bussie, turned from her bed with a grave face and said, "It's a mastoid infection, and it's very serious. You must take her to the hospital at once."

An operation had followed immediately, and the surgeon had come from the operating room looking unhappy and saying, "I'm afraid I can't give you a favorable prognosis. The damage is extensive."

After he went out of the room, Mary asked, "Joe, what did he mean?" I told her he meant that Bussie was critically ill. I did not know then that privately he was telling the nurses and the Sisters that our child hadn't a chance in a thousand of surviving.

Then began our ordeal of waiting for the crisis in Bussie's illness. It came in the small hours one night while I sat alone at her bedside. Mary and my Sister-sister were in a room nearby. I saw that our child — this six-year-old daughter who alone of the first three had survived — was at the point of death. Her pulse fluttered in her throat, was still, and fluttered again.

In that moment, I stormed heaven as I had never stormed heaven before. And suddenly my spiritual agony ceased, and was replaced by an extraordinary and unaccountable happiness. I left Bussie's bedside and hastened to the room where my wife and sister waited. I walked in with a great smile.

Mary looked up at me with half-anguished, half-startled eyes. "What happened, Joe?"

"You can stop worrying," I told her with sublime confidence. "Bussie's going to get well."

"How do you know?"

"I don't know how I know. But I know, I know. *She'll get well, Mary!*"

And I turned on my heel and went back to Bussie's room. But instead of sitting on the edge of a hard chair at her bedside, holding her hand and waiting for the worst, I fell into a big chair in a corner and slept.

I was awakened by the surgeon entering. It was broad

daylight. I stood at his side as he examined the chart that hung at the bottom of Bussie's bed. "Well, what do you know about *that!*" he said in an astonished voice.

"What is it, doctor?"

"This youngster's temperature has come down from 105 to normal in a few hours!"

"Does that mean she'll get well?"

He replied with professional caution: "It certainly does mean she'll get well if we can bring down her white-blood count. It is extremely high. She'll need a transfusion. Can you get somebody to give blood?"

"*Can* I!"

I went to the phone and called City Editor Zehner. He listened for a moment and said, "I'll send the fellows right out."

Presently, six or eight *Sun-Telegraph* men came into the hospital, grinning sheepishly. Shaking hands with them, I asked, "How does Zehner expect to get out a paper? He's almost emptied the City Desk."

"Zehner'll stop publication if necessary to pull your little girl through," somebody replied.

They submitted to tests and waited patiently while their blood was typed. Then those who were selected cheerfully gave a pint apiece. Afterward, they stood around shuffling their feet until at last the young intern who had taken the blood asked what was on their minds.

"Isn't it customary to give a man a shot of whisky after a transfusion?" somebody asked.

The intern brought out a bottle and poured the shots, grinning. The men shook hands with me again, and went back to work.

All but one, that is.

Hours later, I was called to the telephone, and heard the rapid-fire voice of Fuzzy Pfarr.

"Where's Barton?"

"Barton? I don't understand. Isn't he in the office, Fuzzy?"

"Of course not. That shot of whisky triggered him. He didn't come back."

There was a pause. Then Pfarr said in a dead-pan voice, "I've made some inquiries. I know what Barton's up to."

I remarked weakly, "Oh. Do you?"

"Yes. He had a spigot put on his arm, and he's going from bar to bar trading blood for whisky."

My laughter was cut off by Pfarr's banging of the receiver.

That afternoon, the surgeon told me that it was important to get as much liquid into Bussie as possible. "She's badly dehydrated," he said. "If you can get her to take liquids —."

"Does it have to be water, Doctor?"

"Anything liquid."

"Don't worry; I'll get it into her."

I went out and brought all kinds of soft drinks. I came back to Bussie's room and arranged the bottles in enticing rows on a bedside table. Bussie watched me listlessly.

"Would you like something to drink, honey?"

She shook her head weakly.

"Do you want me to read a story to you?"

She smiled.

I selected a book of fables and began reading. When I reached a gripping point in the story, I stopped. "Honey, the doctor wants me to read to you as long as you'll drink something. If you don't want me to stop, you'd better take a sip or two."

She nodded. I poured a soft drink into a glass, put a glass tube into it, and carried the tube to her lips. She took a sip and swallowed.

"Does it taste good?"

She made that little nodding motion with her bandage-swathed head.

"Take another sip."

She did so.

"One more?"

She shook her head, and whispered, "Read."

Through the evening and through most of the night the process continued. At the most exciting points in each story, I stopped and persuaded Bussie to take another sip or two. Occasionally she dozed, only to waken and whisper, "Read, Daddy."

Read, sip; read, sip; read, sip — hour after hour the strange struggle with her illness continued.

Occasionally a nurse looked in at us, smiled, and went away. Early in the morning, she came in, took up the chart from Bussie's bed, and looked inquiringly at me.

"Did she take any liquids?"

I pointed to empty bottles.

She raised her eyebrows. "How much of that did *you* drink?"

"Not a drop."

She stared at me for a moment. Then she said, "That's wonderful. *Wonderful*." She replaced the chart and went out.

A day or two later, I came into Bussie's room and exclaimed in alarm when I saw her head twisting and turning on the pillow as if she were in great pain.

"Honey," I cried. "What's wrong?"

Her head grew still, and she looked at me with eyes that were beginning to recover their sparkle. "Nothing, Daddy."

"Why were you twisting your head like that?"

Her little mouth set in a firm line. One hand went up to the turbanlike bandages on her head. "Daddy, if I'm going to have to wear all this stuff on my head all the time, I've got to make my neck real strong."

Tears came into my eyes. I knelt beside her and put my arm around her. "Honey, did you think you'd be bandaged like that as long as you live? As soon as your operation is healed, the doctor will take the bandages off."

Another day, I arrived in her room to find her sitting up in bed, playing with her dolls and talking to them at a great rate. I knew then that the battle was over. Gratitude pierced my heart — gratitude to God, to the surgeon, to the nurses and nuns, to the men on the *Sun-Telegraph*, to all who had helped by word or deed.

Bussie still wore the turban when Mary and I took her home. Mary held her close in the back seat of the car, and walked anxiously beside me as I carried her up the steps to the house into which we had moved so happily a few years before.

Neighbors saw us, and children began ringing the front doorbell to ask shyly, "How is Bussie?" I conferred with Mary. She enthroned Bussie, wrapped in blankets, on a couch.

The next time the doorbell rang, I told the inquiring youngster, "You go around and tell all the kids that they can walk through the living room and say hello to Bussie."

I will never forget that little procession of children, with their great wide eyes, filing in the front door, saying "Hi,

Bussie," in awed tones, and filing out, while our turbaned little daughter smiled at them.

Not many days later, Bussie returned to the hospital and the surgeon removed the bandages. Proudly, he showed me how well the incision had healed.

Making conversation, I said to him lightly, "There's been quite a discussion among the womenfolks about which saint's intercession saved this child's life."

The surgeon smiled. "I know," he said with dry humor. "When the patient gets well, it's some saint. When the patient doesn't get well, it's the doctor."

I touched his arm. "Don't think for a moment we aren't grateful to you. We'll be grateful as long as we live."

"Don't get me wrong," he replied gruffly, "I know God had a big hand in this." And he departed on his errands of mercy.

15

A great comradeship developed between Joey and me — rather too much comradeship for my taste at times. He would not let me out of his sight when he was awake, and displayed an uncanny genius for hearing me when I entered the house while he slept.

My newspaper work sometimes kept me out at all hours of night, but no matter when I got home, Joey woke and wanted to play. He slept in the same room with Mary and me; we have always kept our children within earshot at all times in their infancy.

I took to keeping my pajamas in the bathroom so that I could prepare for bed out of Joey's hearing. I installed a silent light switch so that there would be no snap to betray my presence. Entering the living room late at night, I would doff my shoes and steal like a burglar up the stairway to the second floor. I slipped soundlessly into the bathroom, closed the door an inch at a time, touched the noiseless switch, undressed with infinite care, donned my pajamas, tiptoed into the bedroom, and lifted the covers to crawl into bed.

In an instant — although I had made no more sound than a moth alighting on cotton — Joey was wide awake, sitting up in his crib and beginning his chant, "Da – da – da," meaning Daddy. Also meaning "Play with me until morning."

I was completely defeated every time. No matter what stratagems I tried, I could not get to bed without Joey knowing. There was only one possible solution – I had to learn to get along with less than a normal amount of sleep. I succeeded in doing that. I succeeded so well that to this day I seldom spend the traditional eight hours in bed.

One night Joey cried for hours while Mary and I, unable to discover what was wrong, took turns walking the floor with him and trying every possible trick to quiet him. At last, in desperation, I telephoned to the young physician who had diagnosed Bussie's illness.

Dr. James Barry lived a few blocks from our house. He came unshaven and tieless, his collar open and his hair tousled. It was about 4 a.m. He took Joey in his arms and put him on the dining-room table for examination. And suddenly Joey's agonized crying, which had continued almost without interruption since midnight, stopped. He smiled at Dr. Barry and tried to seize his thermometer.

Dr. Barry examined the little scoundrel from head to foot. Then he turned to us, grinning. "There's nothing at all wrong with this boy except that he was bored, and wanted somebody new to play with." Whereupon he sat down and played with Joey for half an hour before taking his medical bag and returning home. Mary and I were inarticulate with embarrassment.

This was wartime. Transportation was at a premium, and people were accustomed to seeing men and women boarding buses and streetcars with unusual packages. But surely few stranger burdens could have been carried into a bus than the wooden fire truck I brought home once.

Joey, then about four years old, had a mild attack of scarlet fever, and was quarantined in a room overlooking the side yard. Since I had to keep on working and mingling with people, I was not permitted near him at all. Often I stood in the yard and caught paper airplanes as he sailed them down to me from a window, and tried to sail them back.

One day he called down to me, "Daddy, buy me a fire twuck."

I said okay, without thinking.

That noon, when I went out for lunch, I hurried to a nearby store to buy the fire truck. I discovered that toys were almost nonexistent; all the materials were going into war necessities. From store to store I went: no fire trucks. I told myself that Joey would forget about it.

The moment I arrived home that evening, he called to me. "Did you get my fire twuck, Daddy?" I told him I had tried, "but the man didn't have any." His face fell.

I saw that his heart was set on a fire truck. "Ask some other man, Daddy." I promised.

The next afternoon, after my day's work in covering the news in City Hall, I started out to make the rounds of more stores. After walking many blocks, I spied a huge wooden fire truck in the window of a wholesale toy dealer. It was at least four feet long, and had a seat in which a youngster could ride.

I went in and asked the man in charge to sell me the toy. "Are you a dealer?" he inquired. I looked at him helplessly. "No, but I've got a four-year-old boy quarantined with scarlet fever, and his heart is set on a fire truck. I've looked in all the retail stores. No luck."

I paused. "I'll pay retail price," I offered. "I'll pay more, for that matter."

He shook his head, and put his hand on my shoulder. "Look," he said, "you'll pay me wholesale — not a cent more. For a boy with scarlet fever — why, I feel like *giving* you the fire truck."

"Nothing doing," I said. "I'll pay." I did so.

He wrestled the gigantic toy out of the window and stood holding it while we looked at each other. "I don't have a box for it," he apologized. "And I certainly can't put wrapping paper around a thing this big."

"I'm so glad to have it that I'd walk all the way home carrying it if I had to," I replied. I took the truck from his arms and went out.

People on the street turned to watch me, smiling, as I carried the huge thing along, peering around it to avoid bumping into passers-by. The bus driver looked startled as I got aboard, maneuvering the toy carefully through the open door. For a moment, I thought he might tell me his bus wasn't a moving van, but he only grinned with the tolerance of wartime and waited until I had struggled to a seat before starting his bus. I sat there holding the truck on my knees, trying to avoid staring at its red paint, but unable to see over or around it.

Never have I felt more triumphant than when I walked into the house with the truck in my arms. I basked in the excited exclamations of Mary and Bussie and Betty. Then I went up the steps, put the truck on its wheels in front of Joey's door, and called to him, while Mary and the girls watched happily. He opened the door and I pushed the truck toward him. "Here you are, Joey! Here's your fire truck."

He uttered a whoop of joy and rushed forward to throw his arms about my neck. I fled down the steps, laughing and cautioning him, "No, no, mustn't touch Daddy until the scarlet fever is all gone."

He mounted the seat of the truck and pushed himself into his room, riding it joyfully. Many years later, when Joey was almost as tall as I, I saw the truck, its paint faded and its wheels broken, being carried out of our basement and handed to the rubbish collectors.

Not long after the fire-truck incident, my mother and my ailing father came to live with us. Joey was profoundly puzzled by the partial paralysis that confined my father to a chair all day long. He thought that a grandfather ought to be able to play with his grandson.

Within a year or two, my father, having lived a good life, died a good death — the kind of death that fills the beholders with joy rather than sorrow. His body in its coffin was enshrined in our living room between *torchères* and tall lighted candles, against masses of flowers.

Through the days of the wake, Betty and Joey hardly left their grandfather's bier. They sat together on the kneeler at his casket, and jumped up to greet visitors. They rearranged the Rosary in the dead hands, and smoothed Grandpa's hair when it was disarranged by breezes entering through the opening and closing front door.

One evening when there was a lull in the procession of visitors, Joey took my hand as I stood looking down at my father's face. Gazing up at the candles and the flowers, he asked, "Daddy, is that heaven?"

Gently, I said no.

"But isn't Grandpa in heaven?"

"Yes."

"Then isn't that heaven?"

I knelt on one knee beside him and put my arm around his shoulders. "Joey, when Grandpa died, his soul went to heaven to live with God, because he was good. The soul is the part of us that thinks and loves. The soul can't die. Grandpa's body died. It will stay here in the world for a while. Some day, God will send Grandpa's soul back to his body, and then he will be alive all over. And God will take him to heaven, all of him, to be happy always."

Joey pondered what I had said for a little while. Then he asked, "Will Grandpa be able to walk when God makes him alive all over again?"

"Yes. He won't have a paralyzed leg any more. He'll be able to walk."

"Will he be able to run?"

"Yes."

Joey turned his face to me, his eyes glowing. "Will he be able to run and yell and play Indians with me?"

"Yes. If you want to play Indians, Grandpa will run and yell with you."

"That's good," said Joey.

When Joey was five or six, my younger sister Regina — his Aunt Gene — came to live with us for a few months. Joey found himself surrounded by females, and there were occasional skirmishes between his masculine ideas and their feminine ones.

One evening I came home to find him waiting for me at the front door. "Hi, Joe!" I greeted him heartily.

"Hi, Dad," he responded disconsolately.

"What's wrong, Joe?"

He delved into his trouser pocket and came up with what looked like a huge pocketknife.

"Why, Joe!" I exclaimed. "A pocketknife! That's fine. Who gave it to you?"

His gesture embraced all the world of womankind. "*They* did."

"Well. That's nice."

He looked at me glumly. I put out my hand and took the knife. "Open it," he said disgustedly.

I did so. The blade was of rubber.

"How can anybody cut anything with that," inquired Joe with a vast contempt.

"I see what you mean," I said. I took his hand. "Let's go for a little walk."

We strolled around the yard in the bright sunshine.

"Joe."

"Yes, Dad."

"If I get you a real knife — ."

"Yes, Dad!"

I paused. "You know, Joe, they're afraid you'll cut yourself. Or somebody else."

"I know."

"If I get you a real knife, will you promise not to open it unless I'm with you — until you're big enough not to cut yourself?"

"Sure, Dad."

"Okay, Joe. I'll buy you a real knife."

"Dad."

"Yes?"

"I know where there's a real knife."

"Where?"

"In the house. Grandma's got one. I saw it. It's in her drawer. It was Grandpa's knife.

"That's the kind of knife I want, Dad. I'd rather have Grandpa's knife than any other knife. It's just the right kind."

I stood thinking for a minute. "Well, Joe," I said finally, "we've got to be smart about this. We'll go in, and I'll talk to Grandma. You just listen. Don't say anything."

We went in and sat down in Mother's room. After some desultory conversation, I started to reminisce about my boyhood. Presently, seizing a convenient opening, I asked, "How old was I when I got a whittling knife?"

"Not very old," said Mother disapprovingly.

"Ten?"

"Ten, bosh. I doubt that you were six. I thought your father was out of his mind, giving you a knife at that age."

"Did I ever cut myself?"

"No. No, you were pretty careful. I'll have to admit that."

"Well, I think Joey is old enough for a knife. I wish you'd give him Grandpa's knife."

My mother gasped in horror. I argued, "Joey's just as careful as I was, and he promised never to open the knife unless I'm with him."

She yielded at last and handed the knife to Joey. He slipped it proudly into his pocket, took my hand, and said, "Let's go outside and whittle, Dad."

Not once did he ever cut himself — or anybody else.

Across the alley from us at that time lived a boy named Grant MacKinnon. He came to our house often to play with Joe. Their conversations sometimes were wonderful, because Joe could not pronounce "s's," and Grant was unable to enunciate a "y."

One afternoon on my day off, they stood watching me as I painted the house screens in the bright sunlight. Grant edged closer and closer, until at last Joe put out an arm and brushed him back. "'tay back, Grant," he said. "You'll get 'plashed."

"Say that again," suggested Grant cunningly.

"I said you'll get 'plashed."

Grant drew a deep breath and said loudly, with a vast contempt, "Not 'plashed. S-s-s-splashed!"

Joe said nothing. Presently, however, he and Grant wandered to a bench and sat there aimlessly talking. Then I heard Joe asking, "Where are we, Grant?"

"What?"

"Where are we right now?"

Grant replied disgustedly, "In your back 'ard, of course."

"Where?"

Grant raised his voice. "I said we're sitting in your back 'ard!"

Joe took a deep breath. "Not 'ard. Can't you talk right? It's y-y-y-yard!"

16

SOMETIMES, DURING THOSE YEARS in our first home of our own in Pittsburgh, we wondered ruefully whether we had moved into the wrong house. The children's illnesses were by no means our only problem. Much of the time, their mother was ailing or recuperating. Yet the love that held the family together filled the time with happiness and even with fun. And our tribulations brought their own kinds of rewards, in the deepening and cementing of affections, and in the kindliness of friends and neighbors.

The very day we moved in, a French window — something to which we were not accustomed — swung open in the breeze and flung our canary's cage to the floor. The accident cost the canary his life, but introduced us in a few minutes to people all up and down the street.

The canary's legs appeared to be broken. Mary and I, at wits' ends, conferred while Bussie, her eyes saucerlike, watched anxiously. At last I turned to her and said, "Run around to the houses along the street and see whether you can find somebody who knows something about birds."

She obeyed with her usual thoroughness. Soon our house was filled with neighbors, introducing themselves, sympathizing, but confessing their incompetence to solve our problem. Presently there walked in, through the kitchen and into the living room, the wonderful Mrs. Honsberger.

"Here, here, what's all this?" she trumpeted, and everybody automatically made way for her. She lifted the canary out of his cage, demanded toothpicks and thread, and put his legs in splints. "I don't know whether it'll do any good," she said, "but there's no harm in trying. It's up to God and the canary, now." And she bustled out.

In the morning, we found the canary dead. Before I went to work, Mary and I lined a little box with silk, put the canary inside, and tied the box with pretty ribbon. Then we walked in a little procession into the back yard, Bussie leading the way, carrying the coffin.

I dug a small grave. Bussie laid her canary to rest. I covered the box with earth, and she plucked flowers and laid them on the spot. For years afterward, she cautioned me about the grave every time I began turning ground to plant tomatoes or beans.

Mrs. Honsberger lived diagonally across the alley from us. Her garden was the showplace of the neighborhood, and in the long summer evenings, neighbors leaned on her fence to chat with her while she worked. Once I found her fertilizing and watering a single flower. "Kind of pampering that one, aren't you?" I inquired.

"Yes sir," she said in her clarion voice, going on with her work while she expounded her philosophy. "Yes indeed, I'm pampering it. You know, I always plant my garden in honor of Jesus, Mary, and Joseph. Then I come out here some day and I find a plant that isn't growing as it should. It's not giving glory to God the way a plant ought to. So I fertilize it and water it and pet it for a couple of weeks, trying to bring it along. Then maybe I come out and look at it, and it's still not doing any good. I lean right over it and say, 'So you won't grow, won't you? Then get the devil out of here!' "

And she made a plucking and throwing motion with her hand, in eloquent demonstration of what she meant.

I had never had a vegetable garden, and I went to Mrs. Honsberger for instructions when I decided to plant one. She came into our back yard with her determined walk, and began issuing directions. In a little while, she became annoyed with my ineptness. She flung herself on her knees, seized my seeds and tools, and planted the garden while I looked on helplessly. Presently she rose, dusted her hands, said "There!" and stomped away without giving me time to thank her.

She was well into her own yard before she realized that she had forgotten something. She turned and trumpeted, "Water it!" She walked a few more steps and then delivered her final devastating thrust at my utter incompetence. "With water!" she cried.

I grinned and turned to get the hose. Mary was standing on the back porch, looking at me. "Nothing like getting a woman to do your work for you," she said dryly.

I was unperturbed. I have seldom been without some kind of defense. "Well," I remarked with vast reasonableness, "I don't know how to plant gardens, and Mrs. Honsberger doesn't know how to write. If she asked me to write a letter for her, I'd write it. I wouldn't expect her to do it."

My wife turned and went back into the house with an exasperated sigh.

Never, however, did I reach the heights of ineptness that were scaled by two other men in the neighborhood. One of them never lived down the fact that he erected a forest of wooden poles in his garden for his beans to climb, and then discovered that he had planted bush beans.

The other chap I discovered one day carefully watering and fertilizing a tall, impressive-looking plant. I carried on a desultory conversation with him while he worked. At last I remarked, "Healthy-looking plant you've got there."

"Yep," he said proudly, "been nursing it along all summer. I don't know what it is, but it sure is pretty."

"I know what it is," I told him slyly.

"You do?" He brightened. "What?"

"Goldenrod," I replied, and departed suddenly.

A thousand little tendrils of affection and humor swiftly entwined themselves around us to bind us to our home and neighborhood. I remember the boy who would not mow my grass for pay "because if I do, Dad will make me mow ours for nothing." And the woman the children called the "Dog Lady" because she kept half a dozen dogs in her house and took walks along the alley with the whole pack after dark. And the impromptu musical shows Bussie organized in our garage, thinking up the acts, selecting children to play the parts, directing them, selling tickets, and finally presenting the performance for an audience of congenial neighbors.

I recall the cherry trees foaming into white clouds in the spring. And the annual competition between Mrs. Honsberger and me for the first tomato. Invariably I produced the first one — but what pitiful things my plants bore later in the season, compared with her great red tomatoes almost bursting with their own goodness! Nevertheless, I lorded it over her unmercifully for a week or two each early spring.

I think with affection, too, of the mother along the street

who was afflicted with some physical disorder which forced her to move in a kind of extreme of slow motion; but who nevertheless reared a magnificent family of beautiful daughters and handsome sons.

I remember the little shrine we created in the back yard in honor of the Virgin Mary, amid flowering bushes which in summer burst into almost excruciating beauty. I recall how the children sometimes walked down the hill with me to visit the parish church in the evenings. I envision the piercing loveliness of their little heads bent in prayer, and of their little bodies skipping up the hill ahead of me afterward, going into the sunset as if into a mysterious eternity.

Then in winter our hill was sometimes almost isolated in snow and ice. I think of a Sunday morning after early Mass when I exhausted our supply of ashes and the supply of the neighbors in an effort to make the sidewalks safe for people slipping and sliding down the steep grade toward Resurrection Church. And as Mary went out the front door to go to Mass, I cautioned her, "Be very, very careful. Everything's a sheet of ice."

I closed the door and turned back into the living room. After a few moments, the door opened, and there stood Mary, holding her back and gasping with pain. With the unreasonable anger that we sometimes feel when someone we love is hurt, I scolded her: "I *told* you to be careful!" And she replied with her immense patience and humor, "I didn't fall on purpose, Joe."

I telephoned to a doctor, and presently he appeared — a small, very slender man. He rang the doorbell, I opened the door, and in he walked, bent almost double, pressing one hand to his back. I seized his medical bag from his other hand and cried, "Don't tell me *you* fell on our steps, too!"

He shook his head. "Not on your steps — but on the front porch of the last house I visited before this." Mary and he and I eyed one another for a moment and burst out laughing.

Not long afterward, Mary and I emerged from a symphony concert, chattering gaily, and crossed a street to the place we had parked our car. Mary's toe caught on a curb, and before I could lift a hand, she went headlong. I knelt beside her, saying, "Oh, *Mary* — are you hurt?"

She spoke self-reproachfully. "I'm afraid my arm's broken, Joe. I'm awfully sorry."

At a nearby hospital, she was put to bed. I kissed her good night and went home alone. Next day, X rays showed a minor break. But blood tests showed something much more serious — an inexplicable anemia. A specialist kept Mary in the hospital for several days and sent her home with what seemed like tons of medicine.

Her arm was still in a sling when she was taken back to the hospital a day or two later for an emergency operation for a bursted appendix. The surgeon came to me in her room afterward, before she was brought down, and told me that Mary had a grave peritoneal infection. He was gloomy, saying, "I've done my best, but —"

"You've done your part," I replied. "Now it's up to me to ask God to do what we can't."

I went to the telephone and called Brother Matthew at St. Francis House of Hospitality. "Bro," I said, "call everybody you can think of, will you? Convents, monasteries, all our friends — you know."

"It's done, Joe," he said. "Don't worry about Mary."

But of course I did worry. I sat with her as long as I was allowed. Then I went home to the children. It was strange to pretend to them that nothing much was wrong, and at the same time to tell them to be sure to pray for Mommy.

Betty was oddly depressed. Presently I noticed it, and asked her what was wrong. "Will Mommy only have one arm?" she asked, and burst into tears.

I comforted her. "Of course not, honey. What ever made you think that?"

"Her arm's broken," she said, "and I thought—" She jumped from my knee and ran away. In a moment she was back with one of her dolls. The arm was broken off, and she was holding it in her hand. "I thought Mommy would be like this," she said.

I assured her that it would not be like that, and uttered another silent prayer that it would not be worse.

I went to the hospital early next morning. Long before this, I had perfected the technique of bustling into a hospital as if I were the chief-of-staff, and going directly to any room I pleased. "Making like a doctor," I called it, and often it had enabled me to get interviews for the newspaper despite the visiting-hour rules.

I "made like a doctor" now, strode purposefully to Mary's room, and went in.

She was lying flat in bed. A needle had been inserted into a vein in her arm, and the first drops of a blood transfusion were dripping into the rubber tube. My Sister-sister and another nun were seated at the bedside, silently praying. And Mary looked frightened.

Nevertheless, she smiled at me. But as I leaned down to kiss her, her face turned gray and she began to shiver violently. I turned to Sister Regina Clare. "Look," I exclaimed. "Something's wrong."

My sister glanced once at Mary, rose swiftly from her chair, and walked fast into the corridor. In a moment, she was back with a nurse. The nurse, after one quick look, flicked the needle out of Mary's arm. She had been receiving a type of blood somehow incompatible with hers. Her shuddering soon stopped, and the color returned to her cheeks.

Next morning, I found her half sitting up in bed, the picture of health. "Joe," she said, "what's going on? There's a regular procession of nurses and doctors coming in, looking at me, asking me all kinds of questions about how I feel. What's it all about?"

"Well—how *do* you feel?"

"I never felt better."

"Probably that's the answer, then. They can't understand how anybody with an infection like yours can feel well."

Her brow wrinkled. "Maybe I *ought* to feel ill."

"Bosh. If you never have any trouble except feeling well, you'll be all right."

Presently the surgeon came in, smiling. "My wife," I told him, "is worried because she feels too well."

"Your wife's all right," he said. "It's remarkable. The discharge from the incision has been perfectly clear right along. There isn't the slightest sign of infection, and the healing process is normal. And yet, when I closed that incision, there was a great deal of infection."

That night, the children and I thanked God.

Mary's anemia persisted after she came home. Neither medicine taken orally, nor injections of liver extract, accomplished anything. On my rounds of City Hall, I consulted with the city's health director, Dr. I. Hope Alexander. He recommended a specialist, and promised to consult with some of the best men in the state.

Months went by — two or three years went by — and there was no improvement; rather the contrary. Mary's eyes gradually lost their luster. She moved slowly, and her mind did not have its normal alertness. She was tired all the time. The sheen went out of her dark hair, and the color and youthfulness out of her face. She never wanted to go anywhere. She spent as much time as possible in bed, exhausted in mind and body.

One afternoon, sitting alone at my typewriter in the reporters' room in City Hall, I swung my swivel chair suddenly, lifted the telephone, and dialed home. Mary answered, her voice sounding lifeless and weary.

"Look, Mary, I've been sitting here thinking. I know now what to do. We've been leaving too much of this problem to the doctors. They need God's help. We're going to start tonight with special prayers in honor of St. Therese."

"All right, Joe," she agreed.

"Now, listen, Mary. St. Therese has always helped us every time we asked her. We should have put this thing in her hands long ago. We'll start tonight — and you'll see, everything will be all right."

"All right, Joe."

I would never have dreamed that our prayers would be answered in the way they were. Immediately after we completed the novena, I answered the same telephone in the reporters' room one morning, Mary said, "Joe, I know what's wrong with me. I've just been reading that doctor's column in the *Vandergrift News* —"

I groaned. "Mary! You can't diagnose a case from a news-paper column!"

"Joe," she said firmly, "I'm sure that this column tells what is wrong with me. It describes exactly how I feel. And it's talking about people with a thyroid deficiency."

"But your trouble is anemia, Mary!"

"I don't care, Joe. This column describes me exactly. I want you to call the specialist and tell him about it."

"But Mary! He'll think I'm a crackpot! I can't call up and tell him his business!"

"Joe, please call him. *Please*."

"Oh, all right."

I hung up and sat there feeling like a fool. Then there came upon me a compelling desire to get a nasty job over and done with. I dialed the specialist.

"Look," I said. "You'll think I'm a nut. But I've got to tell you something in order to keep my wife happy. She insists on it."

His voice was calm and cordial. "Go ahead and tell me," he said.

I was still mortally embarrassed. "Well, we've been pray-ing to be shown what's wrong with Mary—"

He interrupted. "I could do with some help in that young woman's case, believe me. It's extremely puzzling."

Haltingly, I told him about the medical column in the paper, and about the thyroid deficiency.

"It would be most unusual if this is the cause of her anemia," he told me. "Nevertheless, I've been thinking of attacking the thing from that angle. It won't do a bit of harm to try."

Apparently what had thrown the doctors entirely off the

trail was the fact that previous examinations had shown Mary's metabolism to be normal. Whether a mistake had been made, or whether a change had occurred in a relatively short time, there is no way of knowing. But now a new test disclosed an abnormal metabolism. Mary was given a few tiny thyroid pills to take every day, and all other treatment was discontinued.

The effect was downright magical. In a few weeks, Mary's blood count was normal. Her youthful appearance returned. She began to speak swiftly instead of slowly and gropingly, and to move about vigorously. I realized the extent of the transformation one Sunday morning as I trudged up the hill with her after Mass. For years, I had been holding myself back when walking with her. Now she stepped along so fast that I complained, lagging a yard behind her, "Where's the fire? Take your time, won't you?"

She laughed joyously, and I think she felt like kissing me right there on the sidewalk in full view of passers-by.

Certainly I felt like kissing St. Therese, the Little Flower.

17

I HAD NOW been with the *Sun-Telegraph* nine years. I had
been rewrite man, general-assignment reporter, feature writer,
columnist, and City Hall correspondent. I had covered, or
at least written, virtually every kind of story known to
journalism.

I had interviewed financiers, artists, literary and theatrical
lions, governors and senators, presidential candidates, ex-
plorers, war heroes, bishops, mothers of fifteen children,
butchers, bakers, and candlestick makers — and thieves and
murderers.

Life had been filled with adventure, excitement, variety.
But I was profoundly dissatisfied. The more I matured in
understanding of religion and of the real purpose of life, the
more I hungered to use my abilities and energies, such as
they were, in the direct service of God.

The words I had learned in catechism, "We are made to
know, love, and serve God," grew taller and taller in my
mind — and they seemed to be growing vaguer and vaguer in
many other minds. I felt a deep need to do my bit to remind
people what existence is all about.

Many negative influences pressed me in the same direction.
I was repelled by the thoughtless uncharity of many news-

paper stories, and by the wallowing in details of lust and crime. Above all, I was revolted by the criminally careless treatment of marriage.

Divorce stories disgusted and angered me. One phrase especially aroused my hatred. Reporters always wrote automatically that somebody had "won a divorce." The truth was that somebody had lost a marriage, lost a romance, lost a vocation leading to God. And the nation had lost another stable family. Another stone had been washed away from the foundations of America.

I knew what marriage was. Every day I saw more clearly what it is — a holy state, a sacrament, a union that ought to be indissoluble, a necessity for any nation's survival. I was furious over the legalized handing of women from man to man, and the cruelty to children involved in the infidelity of parents. I could not — and I cannot now — find words to express my revulsion against the cold selfishness of these betrayals, these treasons against the family which is the original nation, against the home which is the first fortress of humanity.

Repeatedly, I voiced my desire for a change to Bishop Hugh C. Boyle of Pittsburgh, whom I visited frequently. There had developed between us a close friendship and a kind of father-son relationship. He was a magnificent conversationalist, and I had taken to spending hours with him, discussing everything under the sun, and drinking from the wells of his wisdom and humor.

Wisely, he restrained my impetuosity. I wanted to dash off and take any job I could get in Catholic journalism, anywhere. He pointed out insistently my duty of earning a living for my family. He pointed out, too, the good I was able to do in my column of personal opinion, and in the stories I wrote about religious events.

After each talk, I would go away thinking that my mind was made up to stay where I was. But soon the compulsion to make a complete change in my work would return, and back I would go to Bishop Boyle. It was a difficult time for Mary. She loved her home and her neighbors, and she did not want to leave them. Yet she said little, patiently leaving it to me to work out my problem.

One evening, when I came home from work, I found a brief letter — little more than a note — from Bill Dooley — the same Bill Dooley who at Notre Dame had insisted that I be made his successor as editor of the student magazine. He was now in charge of the university's placement service, and the Cleveland Catholic *Universe Bulletin* had asked him to recommend somebody to be assistant managing editor.

"I have no reason to think you want to make a change," Bill wrote, "but I've recommended you. If you're interested, write to Joseph A. Gelin, managing editor."

It was an answer to prayer. I sat down immediately and wrote to Gelin to tell him so. I enclosed a sample or two of my writing. By return mail, he asked me to join the *Universe Bulletin's* staff as soon as possible.

I went jubilantly to Bishop Boyle with the letter. He read it, leaned back in his chair, and looked at me patiently. "Do you know anything about the *Universe Bulletin?*" he asked.

"It's a Catholic paper," I told him.

"Is it solvent?"

I admitted I didn't know.

"Can they pay your salary every week?"

I didn't know.

"What's the paper's circulation?"

I was beginning to feel rather foolish. I hadn't the slightest idea.

Bishop Boyle folded the letter and handed it back to me. "I don't want you to go," he said. "I want you to stay where you are."

My face fell. I kissed his episcopal ring, asked for his blessing as usual, and departed, feeling crushed. When I told Mary what had happened, she said softly, "I'm glad. I don't want to leave."

Sorrowfully, I wrote to Joe Gelin that my spiritual adviser wanted me to stay in Pittsburgh. And I went on with my work.

Perhaps a week later, I received a three-page letter from Francis R. Nally, editor of the Toledo Catholic *Chronicle*. In vigorous prose, he told me about the *Universe Bulletin*, about his paper, and about the Youngstown Catholic *Exponent*, all published jointly. Their circulation was well above 125,000, and they were doing a man-sized job of applying the techniques of journalism to the problem of propagating Christian truth. The letter was impressive.

I went back to Bishop Boyle. He read Nally's letter carefully. Then he sat looking at me for a moment. Gravely, he said, "You really want to go, don't you?"

"Bishop," I said, "I think it's a vocation. I think I ought to go."

He considered the matter a little longer. Then, suddenly and unexpectedly, he said, "Then go with God and in His service."

I rose, beaming, kissed his ring, received his blessing, and ran down the steps of his house. I walked around the corner and telephoned Mary.

I did not really realize as yet her feelings in the matter. "We're moving to Cleveland," I told her joyously. "The bishop says I can go."

There was a long silence. I waited. Finally I inquired, "Did you hear me, Mary?"

"Yes," she said, in a small, faint voice.

"What's wrong, Mary?"

There was another long silence. "Nothing," she said at last, and I knew that she was trying not to weep — and not succeeding very well.

"Mary," I said, and stopped. Presently I went on, "Don't feel that way. I didn't know —. Everything will be all right."

"I can't talk about it now, Joe. Later."

I said good-bye and went out of the telephone booth feeling both happy and blue.

The children disapproved of me heartily. They did not want to leave their home and yard, their school, their playmates. They said little, and their mother said less, but the atmosphere was doleful.

One evening the youngsters came solemnly to us where we sat in the living room. Bussie was spokesman. "This house doesn't have an attic," she said. "We've always wanted an attic. We had a meeting, and we decided we'll go to Cleveland with you if you buy a house with an attic."

"A house with an attic you shall have," I promised them, and they marched away happily.

But Mary was not so easily bribed. She was not to be bribed at all. I was to learn much later — after we had lived in Cleveland long enough for her to fall in love with her new city — that she consented to move only because of her sense of duty and her loyalty to me. "I was brokenhearted," she told me. "I offered it up to God." Then, smiling, "But now I wouldn't want to leave Cleveland for anything."

18

I SUPPOSE THAT A GREAT MANY FOLKS, when they are going through a house with an eye to possible purchase, feel called upon to restrain any enthusiasm they might feel for it, lest they compromise their bargaining position when the time comes to talk price. Certainly this was true of those who examined our house in Pittsburgh after we advertised it for sale.

Not only did they restrain any possible enthusiasm; they disparaged the house at every point possible. Wandering from room to room, they grew gloomier and gloomier, and more and more disapproving at every step. Their remarks annoyed us even as they amused us. We loved that house; we had been happy there, and snug and comfortable. But the visitors grumbled almost as if they were inspecting a noisome slum.

They complained that the living room was too large (or too small). Ditto the dining room. Ditto the kitchen. Ditto the bedrooms. They asked suspicious questions about the plaster. They seemed uniformly convinced that the basement must leak like a sieve. They looked down their noses at the heating system. They remarked in that Certain Tone of Voice that of course the leaded glass windows must be extremely difficult to clean. And there was a kind of horror in the way they observed that the windows were French windows; as if French windows must somehow be subversive. And they didn't even suspect that one of them had administered the *coup de grâce* to our canary! — and that the canary now singing in his cage was our second.

They looked at the big lawns and said that they didn't want to spend all their time mowing grass. They rejected the front steps as too steep, and the stairway to the second floor as not steep enough, taking up too much space. They admitted that the flowering shrubbery might be beautiful in spring and summer; but who wanted the responsibility of trimming shrubbery? They poked around foundations and walls, and voiced dark suspicions about their stability, although they had been standing for a quarter of a century.

Day after day they came and went, sniffing from room to room and piling objection upon objection until at last I remarked lugubriously, "Maybe we'd better abandon the place and move out before it falls down around our ears or sinks into the earth."

So pervading was the air of disapproval that Mary and I felt like a starving man offered food when one house-hunting woman did condescend to admit, as she went out the front door, "Well, the place does have possibilities."

Of course, we heard later that not a few of the disapproving visitors took it as a personal affront when we finally sold the house without first having given them an opportunity to change their minds about disliking it.

The man who at last did buy the house was young and apprehensive. I understood his feelings; he had never owned a home, and now he was facing the frightening prospect not only of investing all his money, but of assuming a mortgage. I sympathized profoundly with him, and with his wife and two small children. I had felt exactly the same uncertainty and fear before buying this same house, six years earlier.

The morning the young man came with his little family to look at the house, the children and I had gone for a walk. We wandered through the fields, inspecting bugs and wild flowers, and finding the skeleton head of a cow. Joey pretended that it was a buffalo, and we kept a sharp eye out for Indians. Strolling homeward, I stopped our little procession, and said, "Let's say a prayer and ask St. Anthony to send somebody to buy our house."

We said the prayer there in the open country and moved on. When we reached home, the young man and his wife were beginning their tour of inspection.

With agonized apprehension and touching simplicity, the young husband said to me several times, "What's wrong with the house?" Each time I explained patiently that nothing was wrong with it; that I had taken a job in another city, and we must move there.

Swiftly, I came to like the little family. We drifted into the outdoors and stood looking at the lawns, the trees, the flowers, the vegetable garden. The young man was suffering a racking indecision. His wife said firmly that she wanted the house. It was just the thing for the children. "They need space like this," she said. "They need the grass and the sunshine."

The young man went on hesitating. Suddenly I decided that we had had enough of house-hunters, enough of waiting, enough of not knowing how long we must live in a house which we knew we must leave. I told the young man, "Look. I want to sell and get out of this city. Your wife wants this house. All right . . ."

Just then one of our children came running to tell me

that another man and wife were inside with another real estate agent, and that they wanted to talk with me.

The young man looked alarmed. His wife spoke his name, softly, insistently.

"Look," I said. "I'm going to lop $500 off the price, if you'll say you'll take the house. If you'll take it, I'll tell the people inside that it's sold. What do you say?"

Now the young man indeed looked tortured. He hesitated. The real estate agent who had brought him intervened. "All right," he said. "If he won't take it, I will. At that price, I'll buy it myself, and resell it. Go in and tell the people it's sold."

The young man uttered three strangled words, "I'll take it."

I went inside and told the other house-hunters that I was sorry, but the house was sold. They went out angrily, asking in injured voices why I hadn't consulted them first. I smiled wearily, shut the door, and went to my desk to sign an agreement with the young man and his wife.

After the papers were signed, I said to him, "You're going to be happy here. This is a good house, a friendly house, a house that kind of watches over you. And it is a happy house. There has been a lot of love and joy inside these walls."

He smiled feebly and led his family away.

A week later, he telephoned. "The loan has gone through," he said. "The house is ours. It's all settled. We can't back out now. So *now* will you tell me what is wrong with the house?"

I think my voice nearly broke as I assured him plaintively, for the dozenth time, that nothing was wrong. But I knew he was still worrying as I said good-bye and broke the connection. Somebody must have told him, some time in his impressionable childhood, that nobody ever sells a house unless something is wrong with it.

19

THE MOVING COMPANY ASSURED US that its van would arrive at 7 a.m. at our house — now the house of the young man who was so sure there was something wrong with it.

At 6, Mary and I — we had finished packing late the night previous — dragged ourselves out of bed and awakened the children.

Before 7, we were ready. We had eaten breakfast, washed the dishes, packed the last few necessities, washed the youngsters, and dressed them in their Sunday best.

We wanted the whole family to look well for the trip to the new city.

The moving men did not appear until 3 p.m. By that time, the children were disheveled, the patience of their parents was wearing thin, and we were all ravenous, although we had munched from time to time on odds and ends of food.

The train was due to depart at 5 o'clock, which meant that we must leave the house no later than 4 to get a streetcar to go to the railroad station. We had no auto at that time; we had sold it because of the wartime gasoline shortage.

At 3:30, I handed the keys of the house to the moving men, who were just beginning to load their van. "See you at the other house," I said.

What perishable meats and bread we had left, we carried to a neighbor. We said our hurried good-byes, promised to write now and then, and started down the street toward the trolley line.

People sitting on their porches called good-byes. We waved and went on, shouting that we had to catch the train.

Mary was carrying a shopping bag. Joey was toting another, smaller bag. Bussie and I were laden with suitcases. Betty carried her canary, Pop Eye, in a cage with a cloth thrown over it.

We looked like refugees fleeing before an advancing army.

We stopped in our parish church for a moment to ask for God's blessing on our new life.

At the railroad station, I asked the ticket clerk whether the coaches on the train we intended to take were new and air-conditioned. He assured me solemnly that they were.

But this was wartime, and I had heard such assurances before. I leaned toward him.

"Look," I said, "I've got my wife and three small children with me. The weather's stifling. If you aren't sure about those coaches, I'd rather take a Pullman, if we can get seats."

He looked hurt. Was I suggesting that he didn't know what he was taking about? "I wouldn't fool you, Mister. Save your money. The coaches are air-conditioned, with reclining seats. You'll be as comfy as can be."

And he looked at me as if daring me, at this point, to insult him by asking for Pullman tickets.

"Okay," I said.

Our coach was "air-conditioned," all right. It was air-conditioned in the sense that it was so hot that the conductor left both doors open. Smoke and cinders poured through in a suffocating cloud as soon as the train started moving.

I said to Mary, "When the conductor comes around, I'll ask him if we can get Pullman seats."

We couldn't.

Betty and Joey wrestled hilariously in their seat. Occasionally their shoes, black with soot, brushed against us. In short order, all of us began to resemble coal miners emerging from the depths.

In addition, I was unshaven.

I told the children to sit still, but Mary said wearily, "Let them play. They've been good. They can't just sit."

Finally Betty and Joey fell asleep, stretched on a seat in front of us. Bussie was across the aisle, absorbed in a book. Mary was nodding. Black, acrid smoke swept through the coach in gusts. Cinders settled in thick films upon the sleeping children, and lodged in my hair, in my eyebrows, below my eyes, on my clothing. My face was smudged and streaked. So were the other faces.

I lighted a cigarette.

I was sitting there smoking and trying to be philosophical when the conductor came past. Over his shoulder, he flung at me the immemorial chant of conductors, "No smoking."

I went on smoking. I finished that cigarette, and lighted another. Inside me, a kind of hot compound of irritation was beginning to boil and bubble.

An analysis of that compound would be interesting to a psychoanalyst. There was resentment in it, and hatred of injustice, and simple annoyance, and a bit of the feeling that, by George, an American is an American, and a citizen is entitled to his inalienable rights, and one man is as good as another, and to the devil with petty tyranny, and so on.

The conductor came back through the coach. He stopped at my seat, put his hand in comradely fashion on my shoulder, and shouted above the rattle of the train and the roar of the locomotive, "Look, son, when I ask you to stop smoking, why don't you stop?"

"Don't son me," I said.

Mary nudged me. I ignored her.

The conductor was taken aback. He dropped his hand from my shoulder. Presently he said, "All right. But why don't you stop smoking? This is a no smoking coach."

I gave him the look of the man who has had just about enough of despotism — a thus-far-and-no-farther look. "This is an air-conditioned coach," I told him nastily. "In air-conditioned coaches, smoking is permitted."

He stared as if I had lost my senses. "This is *not* an air-conditioned coach," he said.

"The railroad says it is," I replied with hauteur. "In the station, they took a solemn oath that it was air-conditioned. So as far as I'm concerned, it's air-conditioned. I'm smoking."

Mary nudged me again, and said in the tone she reserves for soothing her husband, "Joe." I ignored her again.

The conductor looked at me helplessly for a moment. Then he decided to try sweet reasonableness again. "Look," he said, "I'm not the railroad. I'm not the railroad station. I'm the conductor. The railroad makes the rules. I don't. It's not my doing. The railroad says no smoking. Now why don't you be a good fellow and stop?"

I decided to be reasonable myself. I raised my voice still louder over the racket and roar of the train. "Let me tell you how it looks to me," I shouted. "See the smoke and soot and cinders blowing through here? Look at those children." I pointed to their smudged faces and blackened hands. "Look at me." I pointed to my streaked face. "This coach is like a coke oven. And you fuss about a bit of cigarette smoke!"

The conductor paused, gulped, and tried once more. "Like I said," he said, "I don't make the rules —"

"Then forget them," I growled. "I'm going to smoke. Stop the train and put us off, if you want to. If you don't, let me alone." And I turned and stared obstinately out the window.

The conductor cast his eyes heavenward, shrugged, spread his hands, and departed. I sat there thinking that, by gum, now and then we human beings simply have to strike a blow for freedom, and no two ways about it.

Mary sighed and went back to her dozing. Sometimes a wife just can't do a thing with a husband except put up with him.

It was dark when we arrived in Cleveland. Lugging our bags and our canary, we made our way through the great Terminal and out to Public Square, where we hailed a taxi.

I knew the name of only one hotel. I gave it to the driver. In a few minutes we were walking into a brightly lighted lobby.

I approached the room clerk and gestured over my shoulder. "My wife and I and three children," I said. I wondered what he would think of my streaked, smudged, unshaven face.

He appeared to think nothing of it at all. He studied his records, and said with immense courtesy, "We can give you adjoining rooms with five beds, and a connecting bath. Would that suit you?"

"Would it *suit* me!" I replied fervently. I hadn't expected the Presidential suite. I took out my wallet and inquired, "How much will that be?"

He looked at me curiously. "Why do you want to pay in advance?"

"Well," I said, "we don't look very elegant. I thought—"

He flipped a hand. "You look fine to me," he said. "Pay when you leave."

I restored the wallet to my pocket, turned, and stopped, staring at Betty.

She was surrounded by a little crowd of adults to whom she was displaying her canary. Her tight brown curls gleamed in the overhead lights, and her soft eyes were shining. "We call him Pop Eye," she was saying.

The adults were exclaiming over the canary, but they weren't really interested in the canary. They were interested in Betty.

"Beautiful child," murmured a woman to me as I approached. She glanced at Mary, Bussie, and Joey, seated beside Betty. "Beautiful family," she said. "You're a lucky man."

"Thank you," I said. "Thanks very much. Yes, I *am* lucky, and I know it."

"That's the way it ought to be," said the woman. She glanced into my face for a moment, and I thought I detected a sadness in her eyes and voice. "So many men don't know it, you know. Keep on knowing it, will you?" She touched my arm for an instant, and was gone.

In our "Presidential suite" we had a hilarious time bathing the children and ourselves, and donning unsooted and uncindered clothing. I felt like a new man after I had shaved. I entertained forgiving thoughts about the railroad conductor, and even about the railroad, reminding myself that, after all, the railroad people were doing a magnificent job of handling the swollen war traffic, and were setting astonishing safety records.

The milk of human kindness, however, soured in me soon enough. We went down in the elevator and out to the street, and wandered along until we found a restaurant.

The waitress, doubtless another war product, flung everything at us with a clattering and banging, and without even a smile for the children. When we were leaving, I went to where she was standing, handed her a tip, and hissed, "You don't deserve this, and let me tell you, young lady, you'll never be anything but a third-rate hash-slinger if you don't learn courtesy."

She was speechless.

Outside, Mary cocked an eyebrow at me and remarked something to the effect that I must have gone into training to be the Terrible-Tempered Mr. Bang.

I don't remember whether I grinned at her or growled at her. The simple fact was that my nerves were raw and my body nearly exhausted.

And anyhow, conductors shouldn't be unreasonable despots, and waitresses shouldn't throw food at you as if you were a dog.

At this late date, from the vantage point of older and serener years, I will admit that passengers and customers ought to remember that conductors and waitresses get tired, too.

20

IN THE MORNING WE WALKED from the hotel through bright sunshine to the battered old cathedral nearby. After Mass we returned, collected our luggage, paid for the "Presidential suite" and went outside. I piled the family into a taxi, Pop Eye and all, gave the driver the address of our new house, and waved as the cab pulled away from the curb. Then I went to work.

I left my desk early and took another taxicab. My heart swelled as I rode along our new street toward our new house. The children were playing under the trees near a big moving van that was backed into the driveway. Burly men were carrying the last pieces of furniture up the three front steps and into the house. I went along the walk and into the living room feeling like a monarch surveying his kingdom.

Perhaps it was the hours I had spent all alone in that house that had made me love it so soon. There is something profoundly moving about being alone in an empty house, without furniture, without drapes, without so much as a box to sit on; especially if the house is a strange house, and you experience the eerie feeling of being at once both the owner and an intruder.

Every reader will have his own opinion, his own attitude, and perhaps his own experience in the matter of prayer. For myself, I can only tell what had happened. Before I left my family to take up my new work and to look for a new house, Mary and I and the children made a novena in honor of St. Anthony. Each day for nine days, we asked the saint who is known as the Wonder-Worker to add his prayers to ours that we might find precisely the right place to live in the new city, an utterly strange city to us.

The real estate agents with whom I talked after going to my new job looked at me pityingly when I told them how much I could pay for a house. They informed me flatly that I hadn't a chance to find what I needed, in a desirable neighborhood, at any such price. I did not mention St. Anthony, but I replied airily that they were mistaken. I *would* find the right house, for what I could afford. They shrugged and said in dismissing-the-matter tones that they would phone me if anything like that turned up.

With Joe Gelin, I studied a map of the city that hung on a wall of our office. It is a large city — geographically very large — and at that time I hadn't the faintest notion what any of the dozens of residential sections was like. I grew more and more confused. Finally I said, "I'm going to leave it to St. Anthony. I could spend a year combing this city, to no purpose."

I settled down to my work, stayed away from the real estate agents, and left it to St. Anthony — the man who, while living, had been famed not only for his holiness and his powerful intellect, but also for the delight he took in performing the smallest services for his fellow men.

This courteous and considerate saint had carried his personality into eternity. He is known to this day all over the world for helping people in little ways as well as big. He helps them, for instance, to find things that have been lost — often things that are of little but sentimental value.

Often — more often than I can recount — St. Anthony had helped me to find things. He had found for me, in my early childhood, a rosary for which my whole family had searched for days. He had found, many years later, a needle which had been dropped, and which I feared one of my children might pick up. Now I left it to him to find the right house for my children.

A few days after I had "left it to St. Anthony," I got a phone call from Tom Byrne, the same Notre Dame classmate who had telephoned to me from Cleveland to Pittsburgh about Father Peyton. He invited me to his home for dinner to meet his wife Kate and their magnificent children.

After dinner, Tom proposed a little automobile tour. We rode around for an hour, and I had completely lost my bearings when he stopped his car and remarked, "There's a house for sale, Joe."

I looked at the house, and my heart went out to it despite the paint peeling in strips from the outside walls, the untended lawn, and the general air of neglect. I could see, underneath and behind those things, the quality of the building.

"Tom," I said regretfully, "I'm afraid that house would be out of my price class."

"The real estate agent's sitting on the front porch," he replied. "Why not ask him?"

Sure enough, a man was sitting on the front porch in the

sunshine, his feet propped up, a newspaper held in front of his eyes.

I wouldn't have gone in if Tom hadn't been with me. I was sure, as we got out of the car, that it was hopeless to expect to get this house for what I could pay.

The agent shook hands with us and showed us through the house. My heart went out to it even more when we reached the third floor. It was a magnificent third floor — and I remembered how the children had told me that I must buy a house with an attic.

Here was the kind of attic any youngster might dream about.

Back on the second floor, we paused for another look around. With elaborate casualness, I inquired, "How much are they asking for the house?"

The man told me. A thrill went up and down my spine. "I'll take it," I said. "How much hand money do you want?"

"None," said the agent. "You look like a man of your word. I'm going outside and take down the For Sale sign. It's your house. Come into the office some time tomorrow and we'll make out the papers."

We sat in Tom's car and watched while the agent took down the sign, tossed it into the trunk of his automobile, and drove away.

Tom mopped his brow. "Wow!" he exclaimed. "When you go house-hunting, you don't fool around, do you?"

"It wasn't I," I said. "It was St. Anthony." Then I added, "And St. Ann, of course."

Tom turned in his seat to face me. "St. Ann?"

"Yes. We made a novena in honor of St. Anthony, but on

the way out here today, I stopped in a church, and they were having a novena in honor of St. Ann, so I asked her help, too."

Dramatically, Tom asked, "Joe, do you know what parish this house is in?"

"I don't even know what part of the city it's in. You drove around so long that I'm completely lost."

Tom chuckled. "See that street leading away almost directly in front of your house? My house is two blocks down that street. You and I are in the same parish. The church and school are just a couple of blocks farther along."

"What parish is it?" I inquired without much curiosity.

"St. Ann Parish," Tom informed me solemnly.

I signed the papers for the house next day, and afterward, at work, happened to glance at a religious calendar on my desk. It was the feast of St. Ann.

St. Anthony, obviously, is as courteous as ever. He had stepped back out of the limelight, and brought St. Ann forward into it.

The real estate agent gave me a key to the house, and evening after evening I took the bus to our new neighborhood, walked along the street under the tall trees that lined it, opened the front door with that curious thrill which ownership gives, and spent hours poking from room to room while twilight waned and night fell.

The previous inhabitants had left behind them two small electric-light bulbs. By moving these alternately from socket to socket, standing on a rickety ladder I found in the garage, I was able to inspect our new home — perhaps I should say our new kingdom — almost to my heart's content. It is a wonder that our house did not acquire the reputation of being

haunted, what with lights going on and off as I descended
from the third floor to the basement, and then ascended the
way I had come.

St. Anthony had made a cunning selection for us. The
house was to prove itself endlessly adaptable to changing
needs through the passing years. Our friends sometimes
have said that the walls must be of rubber, considering how
many guests we could accommodate comfortably. The basement was so commodious that it provided at once for storage,
for the washing and drying of clothing, for children riding
tricycles and Irish racers, and for television and ping-pong.
And the hall on the second floor proved precisely the right
size for showing miniature movies. Merely by closing the
doors of all the bedrooms, we could darken it in a minute.

I have developed a philosophy of housing; and the first
principle is that a home ought to be large enough to give
everybody an opportunity for reasonable privacy, and yet
small enough to insure family intimacy. There ought, of
course, to be enough land to allow boys to toss baseballs,
girls to skip rope, and a husband and wife to get their fingers
into the soil and bring forth flowers or vegetables. It is good,
too, if there can be a swing or two, and a seesaw, and
perhaps a playhouse.

Certainly a house ought to have a fireplace — a wood-burn-
ing fireplace before which children can lie on their stomachs
in winter while their elders dream into the flames. I do not
think that governments ought to interfere unduly in family
affairs; but I would be tempted to support a candidate for
the Presidency who would promise a law making fireplaces
mandatory in all homes.

And by the bye, I hold that houses ought to have more than

one floor, and if possible three. Otherwise, how can Grandpa or Grandma get away from the energy of the youngsters and the bustling of parents when the noise and the happy uproar become intolerable to aging nerves?

I strongly advocate basements, too. I have known the time when I have seen my wife's father there, exchanging reminiscences with two or three cronies, while on the first floor my wife and I were entertaining guests, on the second floor somebody was napping, and in the attic half a dozen children were playing with dolls and toy trains.

Oh, a house, I tell you, ought to be a kind of principality, with something for everybody. I have even asserted — and I assert again — that every home ought to have its own flag, flying bravely in the breeze, with a star for every member. And it would do no harm if, in the morning, before the day's work began, Father and Mother and children were to assemble on the lawn and stand at attention while the colors were unfurled and raised to the top of the flagstaff. Come to think of it, there are toy trumpets on which one of the youngsters might sound the appropriate strains in that noble moment of family solidarity.

There is one more requirement for the perfect house — perfect neighbors. If possible, every house ought to have the kind of neighbors we have had. We have had the Catholic Torers, succeeded by the Catholic Reilleys. And we have had the Protestant Howards, succeeded by the Protestant Granthams. And then we have had a Jewish family whose name escapes me, succeeded by another Jewish family, the Rickmans, who are with us as this is written. When you are surrounded by people like the Reilleys, the Granthams and the Rickmans — as we are now — well, you do not move.

You would be an idiot if you did. And we have no intention of qualifying as idiots.

Our first evening in our new house was signalized, as was right and proper, with a fire in the fireplace. Never had we had a fireplace before, and repeatedly I cast longing glances at it through the late afternoon while we placed furniture, connected the kitchen stove, prepared our dinner, and generally got settled.

It was September, and the evenings were very long. After dinner I disconnected the gas log that some unromantic soul had installed in the fireplace. Not even the discovery that I had no plug with which to close the end of the gas pipe discouraged me in my determination to have a fire.

I sauntered through a gap in the hedge into the adjoining yard, knocked at the back door of the next house, and mentioned my problem to the Jewish woman who opened it. With immense cordiality, she told me to come in. "My husband has all kinds of tools and fittings and things," she said. "He is always fooling around in the basement, fixing something." Then she raised her voice and called. Her husband appeared, shook hands, listened to my story, and disappeared into the basement.

In a moment he was back, carrying wrenches and other equipment. "Come on," he commanded, and led the way to our house. He squatted down and began working. I protested feebly, but he waved me away. In short order, all was in readiness. "Now," he said, "all you need is some andirons."

"Would one of those steel baskets do?" I asked anxiously. "You know — the kind people burn coal in."

"That would be fine," he assured me.

I went to the door and called the children. They came running. "Scatter around and find wood," I directed. "Old branches, pieces of boxes — anything like that."

"What're we going to do, Daddy?"

"We're going to have a fire in the fireplace."

With whoops of joy, they scampered away. I thanked my new neighbor, drank a bottle of beer with him, and saw him to the door. Then I ascended to the attic, where on one of my exploring tours I had seen the steel basket. I lugged it downstairs and set it into the fireplace.

Mary came in from the front yard and stood watching curiously. "What are you doing?"

I rubbed my hands gleefully. "We're going to have a fire in the fireplace."

She stared. "Joe! The temperature is 85!"

"I don't care. I want a fire in the fireplace on our first evening in our new house."

"But we'll roast!"

"I'll leave all the doors and windows open."

She sighed and went outside.

One by one, the children came with bits of wood and broken branches. It was astonishing how much material they had found.

I squatted, arranged paper and wood in the basket, touched a match to the paper, and stood back. In a few minutes, we had a cozy fire. The children capered in excitement and ran out to tell their mother.

I stood there with beads of perspiration on my face and reveled. This was living.

21

It has seemed to me that the birth of our Jimmy was attended by special divine courtesies. Apparently those old saints of the desert, Anthony the first hermit and Paul the first cenobite, were determined that everything would be done to a T when the child arrived whom I had promised to name for them. And how is it that his name is Jimmy? All that will be explained in due time.

The thing started with one of those conversations between father and son that take place while Dad is shaving. Joey, perched on the edge of the bathtub watching me, was plying me with questions. Presently he said, "Dad, I want a baby brother."

"So do I. I mean I want a baby son."

"Then let's get one."

"Nobody but God can give us a baby."

"Then let's ask God."

I washed the soap from my face, dried, and stood looking at Joey for a moment. I was thinking that more than five years had passed, and no new child had come to us. And here was Joe, asking the same questions, getting the same answers, and responding in the same way, as Bussie had asked and responded years ago, when she was our only living child.

"Maybe God doesn't want to give us a baby," I began cautiously.

"God can do anything, can't He?"

"Yes."

"Well, I want a baby brother. Let's go to church and ask God for one."

"All right."

We walked to St. Ann Church. I entered a pew, but Joey did not follow. He strode directly to the railing in front of a statue of St. Joseph.

I could hear him whispering rapidly. Presently he made the Sign of the Cross and came back to me. He turned his face up to mine and said, "Done." Then he turned and led the way toward the exit.

On the way home, I tried to caution him again with some vague remarks about God not always giving people what they think they want. Joey looked at me, amazed, and said in a rising silvery voice, "I *asked* Him, didn't I?"

"Yes," I admitted.

"I asked St. Joseph, too," he said. "God will send me a baby brother."

Just about that time, the war ended. On the eve of Thanksgiving Day, we were all in the kitchen, and the children were drinking root beer. The telephone rang. I answered, and heard for the first time in more than four years the voice of Jim Flannery. "It's Flannery!" I announced. Root beer sprayed as three little mouths opened to shout their joy.

"I'm in the Terminal," Jim told me. "I'll get a taxi right

away and be out there in a hurry. What's your address?"

Bubbling with excitement, we went into the living room to wait. Alas, we had forgotten that although the war had ended, the taxicab shortage hadn't. A steady rain was falling. The hands of the clock crept around while we paced the floor. The children took turns watching from a window and crying, "Here he comes!" each time they saw automobile lights.

Midnight passed; it was Thanksgiving Day. Still no Flannery.

We hadn't the heart to send the children to bed. We went on waiting. At one o'clock, headlights came along our street and stopped in front of our house. "It's Flannery!" shrieked Bussie, and Betty and Joey took up the cry. We seized umbrellas and ran out into the rain in a laughing cluster.

Flannery — Sergeant Flannery, if you please — staggered as three children flung themselves headlong at him. We gathered his gear and followed the noisy little riot into the house. We pumped Flannery's hand, crying greetings. Presently the uproar subsided. We sat down to chat. And suddenly nobody knew what to talk about. We sat there making desultory attempts at conversation across the gulf of four years and halfway-around-the-world and a frightful war. At last we gave up and went to bed.

Next day was better. Joey strutted around wearing an overseas cap and some insignia that Flannery had brought for souvenirs. Bussie sat adoring the soldier for whom she had prayed for so long. Betty watched wide-eyed.

We sat down to our turkey, gave thanks, and began to eat. It was my job to fill Joey's plate, and there were certain rituals that had to be observed. One was, no gravy on the potatoes. I dumped mashed potatoes on his plate and handed him his fork. "Dad," he whispered.

"Yes, Joey?"

"Gravy. On my potatoes."

I stared at him. I opened my mouth and said, "But Joey, you never—"

"Shhh," said Joey. "Gravy, Dad."

He was not looking at me. He was looking at Flannery.

I shrugged and put gravy on the potatoes. Then I looked helplessly at Mary. She gave me a meaningful glance and nodded imperceptibly toward Flannery. I looked at him, noticed nothing unusual, and raised my eyebrows at her. She lifted her shoulders in a gesture that said, "Good grief, can't you understand?"

I gave it up, and began to pour a little pile of salt on the tablecloth beside Joey's plate. This was another sacred rite. In Joey's mind, there was only one way to eat celery. You dipped the end of it into a little pile of salt, and bit it off. But now he pushed my hand away and said in a conspiratorial voice, "Not on the tablecloth, Dad. Put the salt on the celery."

Now I was sure that the boy had lost his mind. I started to protest again, but he cut me short and nodded in Flannery's direction. I looked. Flannery was sprinkling salt on his celery. And Flannery had gravy on his potatoes. At last I understood.

After dinner, Joey and Betty went upstairs to play, and we sat in the living room chatting. We were interrupted by a little procession, consisting of Betty and Joey, descending the stairway.

They marched in military fashion to where Flannery sat, and stopped. Joey stood straight, shoulders back, head up. "Pardon me," he said. Then the two of them marched back upstairs.

Flannery goggled at me. "What in the world was *that?*"

"Blessed if I know," I confessed. But I determined to find out.

Later in the day, I had a moment alone with Joey. "Why did you come downstairs and say 'pardon me' to Flannery?"

"Betty told me to."

"Why?"

"Because I burped while we were eating, and didn't say pardon me. So Betty told me to come down and say it. So I did."

"Good boy," I said.

When he was out of earshot, I explained the situation to Flannery. He grinned and shook his head helplessly. "Now I want to warn you about something," I said. "For a few days, you'll have to be careful not to turn around suddenly."

"Why?" he inquired in astonishment.

"You'll fall over Joey or Betty. They're right at your heels half the time."

Joey's prayers had been answered; another child was on the way. This posed a problem. If the new baby were a boy, he would have to be named for St. Paul and St. Anthony; we had a promise to keep. But what about Flannery? Something special had to be done to celebrate his safe return from his years of war.

Mary and I talked it over one night after everybody had gone to bed. "We just *can't* not name the baby for Flannery if it's a boy," she told me.

"But he's got to be named for Paul and Anthony," I said.

"Well," she inquired with feminine cunning, "will we name him Paul, or Anthony? Will it be Paul Anthony, or Anthony Paul? Just answer me that!"

"I don't know," I confessed.

"The way to solve the whole problem," she said, "is to name the baby James Paul Anthony. That takes care of everything."

"All right," I consented. "I guess that's best."

The time of fulfillment came in June. On a Sunday morning Mary and I climbed into a taxi as the three children were starting off for nine o'clock Mass. "Pray for Mommy and the baby," I counseled them as I drew the taxi door shut.

In St. Ann Hospital, I parted from Mary and consulted the Sister at the reception desk about Mass. She directed me to St. Joseph Church, nearby. I found it brilliant with lights, beautiful with flowers, and vibrating with joyous organ music. Clearly some special occasion was being observed.

As I knelt waiting for Mass to begin, a procession entered and moving along the center aisle. Priests and altar boys preceded a long double line of Sisters. At the end came a nun flanked by two other nuns, and dressed like a bride.

She was not a young Sister; she was an aged Sister. And yet she looked younger than any of the others. In her face was a glow of joy and goodness. I guessed that she was celebrating her golden jubilee in the service of God. It seemed almost as if God were saying to me, "Stop worrying. I'll take care of your wife and the little one." Peace descended upon me.

After Mass I returned to the hospital to wait and pray. It was Trinity Sunday, and Father's Day. A great lightning storm broke over the city as I sat waiting. Thunder roared, and rain fell in torrents. Then the doctor came to me to shake hands. He was beaming. "You have a son," he said. *"Do you have a son!* Your wife is fine. Now come with me. I'm going to break the rules of this hospital. I want to show you something."

He conducted me to the delivery room, led me inside, pointed to a corner, and said, "Stand right there."

I stood, wondering. A nurse turned and glanced curiously at me. Then she bent over a long litter. I realized with a kind of shock that she was bending over Mary; over my sleeping wife.

The doctor came toward me, holding an infant in his hands. "Look at this boy," he said. "How do you like him?"

I gestured uncertainly. "Is he ours?"

"Of course he's yours! Think I'd be showing you somebody else's? He's yours, and I've never seen a more perfect baby in my life. Stand right there now — don't move. But watch this."

He balanced the baby in his hands, face upward. The little head came up, the strong neck supporting it easily. The doctor turned Jimmy face down, and the little muscles rippled under the smooth skin as the back arched and the head was lifted again.

"Ever see anything like that?" demanded the doctor.

I shook my head, grinning. "No. I never did."

"You bet you didn't," said the doctor. "This boy's as strong as an ox. Now you get right out of here before Sister Superintendent catches us breaking the rule. She'd scold me within an inch of my life if she knew I'd brought you in here. Get out!"

I got out and hastened to a telephone to tell the children and Flannery the good news. "You've got a godson and a namesake; and what a boy he is!" I boasted to Flannery. "You're coming to the hospital right away, aren't you?"

He assured me he was.

As in Joey's case, I had arranged that Jimmy would be baptized as soon as possible after birth. Now I telephoned the young priest with whom I had made the arrangement.

"You caught me just as I was going out the door," he said. "I'm just about to get into my car and start my vacation. I'll be there in the hospital very soon; I'd pass it on my way anyhow. What are you going to name the boy?"

I laughed. "Hold your hat," I advised him. "I'll explain all this later. His name is going to be James Paul Anthony — " I paused — "Mary."

"James Paul Anthony Mary?"

"Yes. There are special reasons for the first three names — and I want to add the Mary in honor of our Lady and because my wife's name is Mary."

"Did you know your pastor's middle name is Mary?" he inquired.

I said no.

"Man," he remarked, "you're putting this kid in solid with just about everybody. I'll be there in fifteen minutes."

I looked at the clock after Jimmy was baptized. He was half an hour old.

Flannery and I stayed at the hospital as long as we were allowed, waiting for Mary to awake, and chatting briefly with her. Then we went outside to go home.

Rain was still pouring down. We stood hoping for a taxi to come along, but our hope was forlorn.

Just then an automobile came along the street, swooped toward us, and stopped. A tall woman reached an arm out to open the door on our side.

"I'm Sergeant Kennedy, Cleveland Police Department," she said. "Can I help you?"

We were almost speechless, but we managed to stammer that we were trying to find a taxi.

"Get in," she said.

We piled into the front seat beside her. She asked where we were going. We protested that all we wanted was to be taken to a bus stop. She asked again where we were going.

We told her Cleveland Heights. "I'll take you there," she said. Ignoring our continued protests, she put the car into gear and sped eastward.

As we rode along, we told her about Jimmy. When she stopped the car in front of our house, we begged her to come in to meet the children. She did so.

Years later, I learned of the magnificent work she was doing with young people in Cleveland, and of the long hours of prayer she invested in them.

Little Jimmy lived up magnificently to the physical promise of his earliest infancy. His days were spent in a crib in our sun parlor until he grew old enough to hold his bottle for himself. Then we moved him into the living room — and this for a strange reason.

The Little Giant, as I sometimes called him, disdained to hold his bottle in two hands. He held it in one hand — his left — and drained it in record time. The moment the last drop had gone down his throat, he swung his arm and the bottle went sailing out of his crib. We were afraid that if we left him in the sun parlor, sooner or later the bottle would break a window.

I wish I could say that, at least once, I was alert enough to catch the bottle in mid-air as it rose in its long parabola from Jimmy's hand. It would be a nice story to tell our future grandchildren — but it would not be true.

22

MARY AND I AGREED, in one of our consultations over the kitchen table after everybody else was in bed, that if we had another child — and if she were a girl — she would be named Regina Marie-Therese.

We selected this name to honor, at one stroke, my younger sister Regina; my Sister-sister Mary, whose name in religion is Regina; Mary the Queen of Heaven — Regina Coeli — and the Carmelite St. Therese, the Little Flower, whose prayers had obtained from God many favors for us and our children.

Neither Mary nor I had ever heard that there is a St. Regina. The thought simply did not occur to us. And this is what happened: the date came and went on which the doctor expected Regina to be born; and she wasn't.

A week passed, and another week. At last the tardy little one put in her appearance.

I came home from the hospital, sat down in the kitchen amid our rejoicing family, and glanced at the calendar. It was the feast day of the St. Regina whose existence we had not suspected.

Regina's birth brought me, so to speak, to full maturity as a father. I waited for her in a parlor where half a dozen young men were sweating out their first such experience.

I sat there calmly assuring them that everything would be all right, and urging them to stop pacing the floor and worrying.

Every time the telephone rang, the young prospective fathers stared at it apprehensively. I smiled, thinking of my own youthful anxieties.

I lifted the receiver, took the message, and enjoyed hugely the privilege of giving the good news to each young man in turn.

Presently, my moment came. I answered the ring and heard the doctor asking for Mr. Breig. "Your wife's fine," he said, "and you've got a nice daughter."

"That's what we expected," I assured him airily.

This time, there was no need for anxiety about getting the infant baptized as soon as possible. The birth was the easiest Mary had ever experienced, and she was so well that she was allowed to come home with the baby on the fifth day, which was Sunday.

Regina Marie-Therese was given her queenly name, and made a princess in God's eternal kingdom, at the age of five days.

Almost before we could realize it, she was celebrating her first birthday. And then her second. And now Mary, with a house full of her own baby-sitters, found herself able to do what she had often longed to do — accompany me on my trips to various cities to deliver talks, or to attend meetings of editors and writers.

At a convention of the Catholic Press Association, we repeatedly received messages that Father Donald Lynch was there, and wanted to meet us. On the last day, we found him — or he us — in the crowd.

I had been doing some writing for Father Donald. He was editor of a little magazine published by the Missionary Servants of the Most Holy Trinity, at that time the youngest religious congregation in the Church.

He was not at all what we had expected from his letters — but then nobody ever is. He was a tall, muscular young man with a face filled with patience and humor, and spectacles that were always sliding down his nose.

The Missionary Servants had been founded by an American priest, Father Judge, who with extraordinary spiritual insight prayed constantly that his little association of priests, Brothers, and Sisters would always be poor.

Father Donald once remarked ruefully to me, "He needn't have prayed so *hard*. Man, are we poor!"

Perhaps Father Judge needn't have prayed at all. He virtually insured his followers' poverty by selecting the poorest of the poor for them to work among — the Negroes of the Deep South and the Indians on reservations.

Father Donald spent week ends and vacations at our house as often as possible. He and I debated constantly and companionably about everything under the sun.

He was profoundly impressed with the religious life of St. Ann Parish. He used to come back to the house after offering Mass in St. Ann Church and sing the praises of the pastor, the redoubtable Father John Mary Powers.

"Any time my arm gets tired distributing Communions in any church," he would say, "I am one hundred per cent in favor of the pastor of that parish. What a man!"

A few years after we met him, Father Donald was transferred to an Indian mission in Mississippi. The study clubs of St. Ann Parish, which he had visited occasionally while at our house, adopted his mission and poured contributions upon it. Father Donald was so overwhelmed that he referred to the clubs as "Charity Incorporated."

Now the wheel of our married life was turning full circle. There began to be seen in our house a young man in constant attendance upon our daughter Bussie, as I had been seen twenty-odd years earlier in constant attendance upon Mary in her home in Vandergrift.

In due time, Terry and Mary came to me where I sat reading at the kitchen table. Mary held out her hand, her third finger significantly extended.

I took the hand of this slender young woman at whose bedside I had once sat wrestling in prayer for her life. I looked at the ring, and it seemed to me that it was a diamond ring. It seemed to me that it was an engagement ring.

And so it was.

I held Bussie's hand for a moment. Then I rose to shake hands with Terry. I was not very articulate at the moment, but I made up for it later by telling of the incident in my newspaper column and mentioning that I had never met a young man I would rather have for my daughter's husband.

I suppose it is trite to say that it was a lovely wedding, but it was. For the second time in my life I appeared in a tuxedo — and this time I was not forced into it by muscular Notre Dame men determined that I must go to a dance and meet girls.

I did object, though, to wearing the double-breasted type of coat. After all, I was no longer the greyhound of a chap who used to ride the fire engines in Vandergrift. The clerk from whom I rented the suit agreed with me.

"You want a single-breasted coat," he said, patting me just below the chest.

"But I've been ordered to get a double-breasted," I replied.

"Just take this single-breasted one, and don't say anything to anybody," he advised.

That is what I did.

On the morning of the wedding, hair tousled, eyes half shut, still in my pajamas, I opened the door of my bedroom and stepped into the hall — and into the midst of a bevy of bridal attendants in orchid gowns.

Well, it was done; I couldn't vanish into thin air. I walked on through them toward the bathroom. As I went, I heard one of the girls say, "Mr. Breig — nonchalant as ever!"

In St. Ann Church, I went forward along the center aisle with Bussie on my arm, and handed her to Terry. Then I turned and absent-mindedly entered the first pew, beside the Flower Girl — our tiny daughter Regina.

We looked at each other and smiled.

A finger prodded me in the back.

I turned my head slightly and saw my wife out of the corner of my eye. She was smiling at me in that amused, affectionate, and slightly derisive way she has with me when I bungle things.

"At a time like this," she whispered, "it is customary for the father to sit with the mother."

I rose, went back one pew, and knelt beside her.

She was more beautiful than on the day we took each other for husband and wife — "two souls whom God has made for each other."

Oh, no doubt she was less beautiful in the conventional — in the superficial and shallow — sense. But another and greater kind of beauty had grown upon her: the beauty of goodness, which one either appreciates, or, unhappily, doesn't.

At the altar, Father Donald was reading in a clear young voice the words of the Church to those about to confer on each other the Sacrament of Matrimony.

"Marriage is a communion of life, physical, intellectual, and moral."

We knelt there, happy. I looked at Terry and Mary kneeling at the altar. I looked at Regina our dainty Flower Girl. I glanced across the aisle at our sturdy Jimmy, the Ring Bearer. I turned my face back to the sanctuary and let my eyes rest for a moment on tall, dark Joe and pretty Betty among the bridal attendants.

I was content. And I could feel contentment flowing from my wife at my side.

I listened to Father Donald's voice invoking the ancient benedictions of the Church upon my daughter and her husband.

My throat closed for a moment when Bussie and Terry rose and walked together to the altar of the Virgin Mary. Bussie laid her bridal bouquet there, and they knelt to dedicate their marriage to our Lady.

I blew my nose.

Everybody, I am sure, repressed a smile. Everybody in St. Ann Parish knows my honk. St. Ann's folk remark to me, "Well, I hear you were at the 10 o'clock Sunday."

They don't mean they heard it from somebody else. They heard my bugle blowing.

My wife nudged me to be quiet. But when I turned to look at her, her eyes were moist.

We formed in procession and left the church — Terry and Mary, Joe and Betty, Jimmy and Regina, Mary and I.

We toasted the newlyweds at breakfast, and hastened home, for the wedding reception, to the house through which I had wandered on those lonely nights, transferring an electric light bulb from socket to socket.

The "rubber walls" did their duty nobly, as always. Hundreds of well-wishers came and stayed and chatted. They overflowed into the basement and into the back yard, in front of the shrine of our Lady and beside the little shrine of St. Joseph, her spouse.

There was room for everybody.

The golden day sped into the afternoon. Somebody summoned me. Terry and Mary were ready to leave. Mary and I shook hands with Terry, and kissed Mary.

We went to the front door with them and saw them into their Chevrolet. Mary handed them a box of goodies, as her mother had handed a box to us in the Ford.

Terry let out the clutch, and they sped away into the sunlight, into their tomorrows.

I put my arm around my wife for a moment and drew her to me. We turned and went back to our guests.

23

As I WRITE, Terry is in the army, and Bussie is at home awaiting the moment when she will give us our first grandchild. Here we are, then, gathered in our living room or our kitchen, holding the world together.

Yes, holding the world together; for the world is held together by united families. The world is held together by love.

Mary and I will be grandparents. And Jimmy and Joe will be uncles, and Betty and Regina aunts. And Terry and Mary a father and mother.

Life — the beautiful, wonderful, awe-inspiring torch of life — is being handed along, and with it, the blessings that God sends forth upon marriage.

About the time this book is published, Mary and I will be celebrating the silver anniversary of our wedding.

We will be kneeling at the altar in St. Ann's, and Father Donald Lynch, the sort-of-adopted priest member of our family, will be receiving the renewal of our nuptial vows.

And he will be giving us again the great blessings of the Church.

We will see Father Donald as we kneel there, but we will see also the bowed head of patriarchal old Father Edgar, the Benedictine monk who blessed us on that first day.

Our children will be kneeling around us, and we will hear the ancient benedictions again.

We will see and hear Father Donald, and we will see again the bowed white head of Father Edgar, and the lifted blue-veined old hand. We will seem to hear again the aged voice praying, "Bless, O Lord, this union, and from heaven watch over it . . . "

Across the quarter of a century, the words will be spoken again.

> *May the Lord God bless you with the fulness of His benediction; may you see your children's children even unto the third and fourth generation; and may you attain to a happy old age. Through Christ our Lord.*
>
> *May the God of Israel join you together; and may He be with you . . .*

This time, we will not be a couple of thoughtless young-sters kneeling at the altar. This time, we will really appreciate the magnificent blessings.

> *And now, O Lord, make them bless Thee more fully . . .*
> *Thy wife shall be as a fruitful vine on the sides of thy house. Thy children as olive-plants round about thy table.*

Mary and I, who conferred upon each other the Sacrament of Matrimony, will bow our heads and join hands and hear the final splendid benediction:

> *May the God of Abraham, the God of Isaac, and the God of Jacob be with you, and may He fulfill His bless-ing in you: that you may see your children's children even unto the third and fourth generation, and thereafter may*

you have life everlasting, by the grace of Our Lord Jesus Christ.

We will see and hear Father Donald calling down blessings upon us.

And then we will seem to see not Father Donald, but venerable Father Edgar.

And then we will seem to see and hear, not Father Donald, and not Father Edgar, but Christ.

We will see and hear Christ in His priest as He blesses us:

That you may see your children's children . . . and thereafter may you have life everlasting. . . .

May it be so.

POSTSCRIPT: The grandchild is a girl. Name of Mary Jo. Born Easter Wednesday. Baptized six days later. Mother and daughter doing fine — as are the father, grandfathers, grandmothers, and assorted uncles and aunts, thank you.